Tea in the Burlington

A MEMOIR

Tea in the Burlington

A MEMOIR

Martin Swords

*Well remembered bits of life. A memoir of an Irish childhood, in the Ireland of the 1950s and 1960s, family, school, and growing up, with a few dramatic twists and discoveries along the way.
Life looks different looking back, if you know the story.*

Tea in the Burlington

Martin Swords

This collection published November 2021
Copyright © Martin Swords

All rights reserved. This book may not be reproduced in whole or in part by any process without written permission from the copyright holder.

Published by Martin Swords
swords.martin@gmail.com

ISBN: 9798486920196

Design: Alan Pepper and Martin Swords
Set in 14pt Baskerville.

For Jacinta, for Kathleen, for May

Memoir Introduction

This Memoir is as we say here in Ireland 'all over the place'. You will see this as you read it, but don't worry, you'll get it soon enough. There is a reason why it is this way. About halfway through my life I learned a significant piece of new information which changed how I saw things in the past, and in the future. This meant that the memories and events of the past occurred in my old, and incorrect state of knowledge, yet I was retelling them here now in a new and correct state of awareness. I see events in the past differently now that I know the story.
The future is different because it carries a changed past. The fact that my memoir starts twenty five years before I was born should not surprise you. Enjoy.

Memoir Thoughts

To the children who were in Temple Hill, Blackrock,
I hope you found your Mammies.

To the children of the many Mother and Baby Homes all over Ireland, I hope your Mammies found you.

To the parents who felt compelled by society and church to place your daughters and grandchildren into these places, to be bought and sold, to be scattered all over the world.
A sense of shame you weren't stronger.

To the church and clergy who encouraged parents in shame to follow this course because in your view there was only one big sin, sex.
You were wrong.

Perhaps the only significant achievement in my life, has been making it this far with my wife Jacinta, sons David and Mark, and their wives, daughters in law Fiona and Naomi, and our wonderful grandchildren, Seán Mark Swords, Julian David Swords, and Charlotte Kathleen Swords.

Children, this is your Grandad telling you a story. You may not read this story for many years, until you are grown up. I may not be here then to answer your questions. If you need help, follow the best advice, ask your mother.

In putting this Memoir together, special thanks are due to my cousin John Goggins, for being close since we were babies as 'pram brothers' and whose research and Family History discoveries drove this story on, otherwise we might have had very little to say.

Contents

A Bit of a Dancing Lesson	11
A Bit of a Daring Move	19
A Bit Romantic	30
A Bit of Disappointment	34
A Bit of News. A Big Bit. Tea in the Burlington	35
A Bit Stunned at the Tea in the Burlington	42
A Bit of Unexpected Conversation, with Tears and Tea	45
A Bit Complicated, Being Born Again	55
A Bit Frightening in the Storm	67
A Bit of a Near Thing Around the Corner	74
A Bit of Growing Up during Some School Days	82
A Bit Better at Some School Lessons	90
A Bit Better at English Class - *The Listeners*	100
A Bit of a Fight	106
A Good Bit of Music	110
A Bit Unexpected	117
A Bit Late for Kathleen	121
A Bit of a Message	125
A Bit of Unusual Activity. On the Nightlines Booterstown	130
A Bit Brave or What?	135
A Bit of a Great Time. When We Were the Boys. The Boy's Club	139
A Bit of Outer Space. From Sputnik to Mars	159
A Meeting that was a Bit Mysterious	163
A Bit of a Mystery	168
A Bit of Omerta. A Good Bit	174
A Bit of a Dip into the Diddley	181
A Bit Sick on the Bus. Again	184
A Bit of a Struggle with Saint Patrick's Guild	188
Another Bit of a Struggle, This Time with TUSLA	196
A Bit of a Chase Around the World after Francis Sydney Byrne	207
Regrets? Just a Bit	236
Notes and Letters	247
Poems arising from this Story	285

A Bit of a Dancing Lesson
Dancing in the Kitchen   mid 1930's

"Dah......Dah.....De...Dah......Dah..Dah..." she hummed to herself as she moved smoothly around the kitchen on the red linoleum covered floor. Her eyes half closed, she moved to the music in her mind, as she twirled, she held one arm slightly raised, at an imaginary shoulder height, the other arm curved, waist high, in an imaginary man partner pose. She continued her dream dance until she was interrupted by the lifting latch as the back door opened. Her brother, weary from work, shuffled in. "Any dinner ready?" his question, weariness and unwashed presence bringing reality back to her dreamy dance.

May loved to dance.

Really loved dancing. So did all the girls, the friends from The Cottages and The Avenue, Maeve, Rose, Agnes, Anna, Aggie and Mollie. Some danced well, others not so, all having little time for learning or practice, what with a busy rota of cooking, cleaning and child minding in each family home. Not their own children mind you, but all the girls were in large families in small houses, often without dads or mams or work, or sometimes all three.

The girls were all good friends, all around their early twenties.

Some worked, in laundries, as assistants in shops in Blackrock, or as catering helpers in the local convent for the nuns who ran the local schools. None were at school or college studies themselves, having left school early, some after primary school, to go to work of any sort as quickly as possible to bring something into struggling families. Wages were small, work was hard and long and there was very little income they could call their own. There was a little though, for girls' essentials, but clothes, dresses, fashion were scarce and a great deal of recycling and remaking of hand-me-downs went a long way. Knitting, sewing and making skills were in every family, some very skilled, so surprising results could often be produced.
Not all the learning was school learning, and not all the resources needed involved money. And there were sometimes bonuses; there were often the remains of large beef joints and bowls of dripping from the convent kitchens, or damaged clothes and material from a shop or laundry. A pair of drape curtains or sheets could be skillfully turned into something wonderful to wear, in the right hands, by one or two of the girls. Even the humble flour sack could be put to many uses, but you wouldn't want to be telling everyone about it.

May didn't work outside the home as there had been some problems in the family, her mother had died early and May as the oldest had been pulled out of school earlier than most to look after the young kids at home. School stopped, but learning of a different sort continued in the school of life.

So for all the friends there wasn't a lot of fun and frivolity in their lives. But there was some, music on gramophone records, on the radio and at family parties where someone could always play a fiddle or accordion, and do a turn. And with music came dancing. Mind, the fiddle and accordion made for jigs and reels, while May and the other girls preferred a piano, or the radio and gramophone music for their choice of dancing – quicksteps, foxtrots and slow waltzes. They could dance the jigs and reels, but associated these with their grandparents and a poor life, and while the girls didn't have much they had modern attitudes and wanted to dance the modern dances to the songs they heard on the radio.

All too often they knew the names of the dances, but didn't know the steps.

But someone among the girls did, or worked with someone who did.

There wasn't a lot of dancing at dances, simply because there weren't a lot of dances to go to. But occasionally a dance was held at some local parish hall, or in a hotel, though hotels were a bit above the girl's social status. No Hunt Balls or gliding across the floor in The Shelbourne Hotel for these girls, in fact most would never set foot in The Shelbourne in their lifetimes, unless maybe to serve at table, and even that unlikely. No, most of the dancing for May and the girls was done in one or other of their houses, pushing back furniture and in bare or stocking feet to glide on the smooth lino floor, while someone who knew the steps taught those who didn't.

Not all the girls were together all the time, but often three of four of the gang would find themselves together in one or other of the houses, simply enjoying each other's company, swapping gossip, recipes or knitting or cookery tips, all useful things to know in their drudging lives at home, their lives of hard work in their roles as assistant mammies, or nearly mammies. But it wasn't all drudgery and the girls needed a little fun in their lives. So there was also some ribbing and teasing and talk of boyfriends, and who looked at who during Mass, and who might fancy who. All the girls knew that most of this talk was fantasy or bravado and while they might in their dreams like to hold hands with Johnnie, or steal a furtive kiss from Paul, they each knew they would run a mile from any boy who made a move. Dancing and a desire to glide gracefully and confidently around the floor was a way to fantasize. The perfect way to realize a dream life, like the dream life they saw when they went to the pictures, or the fillums as they called them. All the men were Fred Astaire in the girls' dreams, and each girl was Ginger Rogers in their own minds. The pictures offered a vision of slim tuxedoed men and dream - figured glamorous beautiful women, so far removed from the girls' humdrum lives as to be like a fairytale, a dream, desirable, but unrealizable.

Meanwhile there were steps to be learned and poise to be practiced. In a spare few moments in someone's house someone would suggest a dancing lesson. Room would be made and a gramophone record put on, usually the same one played over and over and over, there not being a lot to choose from.

Now girls this is a foxtrot so pay attention, it's quite different to the slow waltz we did the last time'. Whoever had taken upon themselves to teach, simply because they knew, or thought they knew the steps, led the lesson. Others followed every move and step closely, eager to master yet another dance. May watched carefully, she was an eager student and had a good sense of movement and rhythm and loved the flow of a dance and how it naturally matched the movement of the music. But she wasn't a teacher as she lacked any desire to be a leader, but was a natural follower.

There were the usual arguments about 'you be a man and I'll be the lady' followed by protests of 'I'm always the man, I want to learn to be a lady'. Over and over the music played and the couples danced, staggered and stumbled into some pattern that began to resemble an acceptable dance, despite the titters, laughs and complaints, as toes got stood on and feet tripped over feet, often their own, but also other dancer's feet. Despite it all steps were learned and a flowing expertise was picked up to the point where the girls felt they really were dancers. It was a great feeling of having learned something worthwhile. All the girls hoped that they would remember the steps when next they heard that song or something like it.

Sometimes a foxtrot, sometimes a two step or waltz, over time a variety of steps were learned. But times were changing and the girls didn't want to be only dancing the dances their mothers or even their grannies danced. The girls thought of themselves as modern and wanted to dance modern dances, to the type of music they were hearing more of on the radio. More and more they were hearing 'swing' and 'jazz', new sounds that were moving, exciting, and made you want to move your hips in a very unladylike way. The kind of music that made you want to get up and dance, even on your own. Times were changing too in the girls' own minds, and bodies, and some began to be more concerned with the 'fella' they might be holding in the dance rather than the steps of the dance itself. Particularly as most of the fellas they knew could hardly put a dance foot in front of them, never mind sweep the girls off their feet like in the pictures. 'Footless' might describe most of the lads, in every sense of the word. Self confidence was often thin on the ground with many of the young men, and sometimes had to be boosted by a pint or a 'Baby Power' especially when it came to meeting girls, never mind dancing.

"Will you put the kettle on itself, till I have a bit of a shave", said her brother, "I'm going to meet the lads in Dwyers to play rings", helping himself to a plate of mince stew. "Able to fill a plate of dinner but not able to fill a kettle and put it on the gas", said May to herself, " you'll be a great catch for some poor young wan".

This little exchange quickly brought May's thoughts back down to earth, far from swing, glamour and smooth stepping couples in the pictures.

May poured herself a plate of the mince stew, a small plate mind you, smaller than his, as she wanted to stretch the stew dinner out into another day. She sat at the table opposite him, the table covered in an open spread of the Evening Press from last week.

Two thick slices of turnover accompanied the stew, for mopping up. They ate in silence. "For God's sake", thought May, "is this it, is this all there is stretching out ahead of me". There was little to cheer her up, not even the soft white turnover.

"If you're going for the few pints with the lads", she said. "You must have got paid, don't forget to put the few bob in the teapot so, before you drink it all."

"There's talk of a bit of a dance coming up down in Bucky's, I'm hoping to go with some of the girls, but I haven't got......". She didn't finish.

"Have you got 'er a few bob to spare, for stuff like"? She thought this might be a good time to ask. To her surprise her brother fumbled the change in his pocket and handed her five bob, two half crowns. "It's all I can spare at the moment, apart from the teapot money. Is the kettle right yet?" "It is so", she answered. He stripped to the waist, had a splashy sort of a wash at the sink, checked the blade in the razor wasn't too blunt and set to to shave. May cleared up to wash the dishes when he finished, pleased with herself for asking, she hadn't expected to get any money at all.

Mary Mahon (May), right, with her good friend Rose Pluck.

A Bit of a Daring Move
Foxrock and Mount Merrion's Best   late 1930s

Word came around that the dance was coming. The girls were all excited, looking forward to it. May hoped to go to it with her two friends, Rose and Aggie. The dance would be held in the large opened-out room of one of the boy's National Schools, near Blackrock, off the Rock Road, not far from Booterstown. May had not been to one of these real local dances before, only to party dances in pubs where the girls usually danced with each other. She'd heard the girls talking about the local dances and saying they were great. They were run by Bucky Devine himself, a local character everyone knew, not so much to make money but to provide a safe, even Christian way of getting the young people together in a well run event rather than a seedy or unsavoury unsupervised dance like in some of the dancehalls in Dublin. The whole thing was organised and run by Bucky, the hall, the music, the lights, stage, and the mineral bar run by Bucky's wife Clarice. A shilling at the door, 'don't expect too much, and you won't be disappointed' might have described it. The Ritz it was not. No glamorous ballroom, no tuxedoed ten piece band on stage led by a Duke Ellington type of bandleader. No, it was just Bucky on stage with a big sideboard-sized gramophone and a box of records, mostly '78's. They were picked by Bucky, played by Bucky, and introduced by Bucky using the old fashioned microphone he had salvaged somewhere. He was M.C. for the night, calling the dances and cajoling the dancers to keep moving in a stream around the floor, and to keep a respectable distance between couples. He would call the dances, the lady's choices, and shout encouragement to the reluctant lads and shy wallflowers to get up and dance.

He also called the breaks between sets, and sent people over to the mineral bar to buy refreshments from Clarice, all minerals, no alcohol. Bucky ran a respectable dance and tried to ensure that everyone got involved and enjoyed the dance, no one left out, many of the girls danced together around their handbags, there was always more girls than lads. All this May had heard from the older girls, it was all ahead of her, and a great deal more though she didn't know it yet. But there was a problem, she didn't have a nice dress to wear to a dance apart from the pinnies and poor dresses she had for scrubbing the doorsteps or going to the shops. What would she do? Rose and herself talked about nothing else other than the dance and a dress. Rose said she might be able to help with the dress but there was a favour Rose needed from May for the dance. Rose, who had seen more of life than May confided in her, 'there's a fella I know from Glasthule coming to the dance, I've heard in a roundabout way, his name is Peter, I've met him before and I want to meet him again at the dance. He says he'll come if he can get a friend to come with him. I want you to dance and chat with Peter's friend, so I can spend time with Peter'. 'Ok sure' said May 'but you know I've nothing to wear, so I'm not sure about the dance at all'. 'Don't worry about the dress, we'll think of something.'

The something Rose thought about involved May's younger sister Ann, who Rose knew well.

Rose and Ann hatched a plan for May. Rose and a few of the girls worked part time, and Ann worked full time in IMCO, near Merrion gates on the Rock Road. IMCO was one of the largest laundries and dry cleaners in Dublin, very busy all the time. Times were hard and getting clothes cleaned and laundered was a luxury. Certainly the likes of May or Rose or Ann did not get clothes cleaned, they washed and ironed them themselves, or they stayed dirty. No, the clothes which were sent or brought in to IMCO came from a very well heeled clientele, and mostly from the better off parts of the Southside, places like Foxrock or Mount Merrion. These clients usually had their clothes collected by the laundry driver and brought in for cleaning. Sometimes the ladies, mostly ladies, called in to leave or collect and the girls got to know them to see, but rarely to talk to. The ladies were well dressed, aloof and haughty with a superior or classy air about them, and tended to look down on the girls in the laundry. They had money, or at least their solicitor or doctor husbands had money. The ladies dressed expensively and as the girls would say they had 'notions' to match their married status, even if they had had more humble beginnings. Some had a nasty superior attitude. 'All plate and no dinner', or 'all fur coat and no knickers', the girls in the laundry joked about some of them.

They were known as 'Foxrock Fannies' or 'Mount Merrion Marys', but their clothes were beautiful. The plan involved spiriting away some of their cleaned dresses for the girls for the dance. Taking them home maybe on a Thursday or Friday evening, sneaking them back in on Monday and putting them through the cleaning process again, for collection later in the week as arranged. Ann and Rose had to warn the other girls to take great care with the borrowed dresses, to keep them clean. Minerals or other drinks might be spilled on them. There might be stains from lipstick or makeup, or pulled stitches, which could be cleaned or mended on return. After all, the name IMCO stood for The Invisible Mending Company. The biggest danger was cigarette burns. All the lads smoked, a lot, some even while dancing. A cigarette burn would be a disaster and in such a case a dress might have to be 'lost or disappeared' never to be found again , there would be hell to pay with managers and probably costly compensation paid to the client, who really didn't need the money. Besides, the managers usually knew what was going on, and often benefited from the same ruse for their own wives or girlfriends. All on the QT.

The girls, and the borrowers, knew each other's sizes and styles, and quietly the selected dresses were spirited away at the end of work. By the time May and Rose and the others were ready to go to the dance on Friday night, they were dressed to the nines and looked fabulous.

'Don't forget May what you promised about Peter's friend', said Rose as they left for the dance.

They arrived in the boy's school hall as the dance was starting up, Bucky was up on the stage calling and cajoling, Clarissa was all set at the mineral bar. The room was filling and getting warm and sticky. Some of the girls were starting to dance, with themselves, around their handbags at their feet. There were hardly any fellas in the room, too early. Almost the first thing the girls did was to congregate in the Ladies to chat and gossip, touch up make-up and straighten stockings. Some of the daring girls had a cigarette, sometimes for the first time. A few had a 'Baby Power' or a naggin of gin. Talk was of who might be there or if 'yer man' from the last dance would be there, 'he was gorgeous'. There was no making use of the toilets for what they were designed for. That and other uses would come later. There were no 'boys' toilets, no mixing, the lads went outside or anywhere they liked.

By the time the girls emerged the hall was filling up. Some of the lads had arrived, more people were dancing, even some fellas. Bucky was in full swing on the crackly microphone and the gramophone was belting out some swingtime. Rose was looking around anxiously for Peter's appearance, but no sign yet.

A long enough time passed, during which Rose began to think that Peter was not going to arrive. Then, while Rose was dancing with all the girls, Rose grabbed May's arm saying 'look, he's here'. They both looked at the door, at the pair of fellas coming in. 'That's Peter, and that's his friend with him I think'.

Rose dragged May off the floor and headed over to meet Peter and his friend. Rose was so keenly anxious to meet Peter, she was beaming. There were warm greetings all round. 'Peter, this is my best friend May, she's a great dancer'. 'Pleased to meet you May,' said Peter with a warm handshake. 'And this is my good friend Pat', said Peter introducing Pat to Rose and May, 'Pat,' said Peter, 'Pat Swords from Glasthule'. Peter, who was shortish, wirey, with tight wavy brown hair, looked up at Pat while introducing him. Pat was taller than Peter, with a long face and dark hair. May saw that he had a beautiful warm smile, a wide smile with a mouthful of prominent teeth, some of which were discoloured. He had a lovely gap between his two front teeth when he smiled. 'The Swords Gap' was a feature running through all the Swords family she would learn. Both Peter and Pat smelled of cigarettes and drink, but all the fellas did then.

There was a little awkwardness for a short while, no one knowing quite what to say. In the awkwardness as they thought of what they would say, or not say, May thought 'he'll do lovely, I hope he can dance'. Pat thought 'a great dancer', 'well that's me finished, but she's lovely'. Pat said to May, 'lovely dress May', unexpectedly, surprising both himself and May, but she was proud as punch to hear him say it. 'That's nice', she thought, 'he's nice'. Rose noticed. 'Right you, on the floor', said Rose to Peter, 'this dance is nearly over', and off they went leaving May awkwardly with Pat. Pat and May were stuck with each other and made a start at a stilted conversation. Pat's warmth helped May get over her shyness, she liked that. She explained that she loved to dance but didn't get to dance often. Pat explained that he worked for The Irish Lights on the Granuaile ship visiting the lighthouses and lightships, and was away at sea regularly. 'Mmmm...a sailor', thought May, 'that's nice, steady'. They talked about their families, brothers, sisters, work and interests. In a lull in the conversation Pat asked 'will you dance so?' May thought he'd never ask. As much as May loved to dance she soon realized Pat didn't, or couldn't. He was awkward, ungainly and sometimes clumsy. He didn't seem to have that innate sense of rhythm and timing to fit to the music, which May had. They struggled on and only bumped into a few other dancers, or stood on each other's toes occasionally. He was a bit clumpy where May was light and skippy on her toes. But May remembered all those lessons where she had had the role of the man in a couple. Unnoticeably she took over the lead role and steered them both around the floor without too many mishaps. Pat was no Fred Astair to her Ginger Rogers. However what she soon realized, and loved, was how much she liked being held in his arms, she felt warm and protected. 'This is new and nice', she thought.

At the interval Pat asked 'will you have a mineral, so?' She agreed. She thought she was in love.

There were more dances, Rose with Peter, May with Pat. May looked around at the other dancers, some gliding gracefully with the music. Some of the girls danced with each other, still looking graceful with flawless steps, remembering what they had learned in the 'kitchen classes'. May would have liked to have been dancing even with one of the girls, swirling round the floor like dancers in the 'fillums', instead she was clumping around with Pat. Still, she liked this new feeling, nearly as much as dancing. There were breaks between the sets and often the girls moved in groups to the Ladies, to gossip, smoke, praise or criticise their dancing partners, 'yours is lovely' or similar was often said. Others wondered would any fella at all ask them up to dance, not showing how much they were hurting. Some of the girls used the toilets properly, others used them to throw up in, a combination of nerves, heat and maybe gin. Some did not make it to the bowl, a real danger for anyone wearing a 'borrowed' dress.

The fellas moved towards the mineral bar, then moved outside the hall with their minerals into which they emptied a naggin of Jameson or Sailor Dark Rum, not being too keen on plain minerals. Nearly all the fellas at some time outside stood at the back wall, for relief. Like the girls the fellas talked about their dancing partners but in a different way to the girls, jokey, slightly rude and lacking the grace and dignity of the girls' chit chat. 'Don't think much of yours', a joke but not a joke, or 'yours is a cracker, does she have a sister' was heard with loud laughter.

The girls and the fellas heard Bucky call that dancing was starting up again and this one is a 'ladies choice'. Rose sought out Peter who did not seem too keen to be found. May found Pat in a group of lads. 'C'mere you' she said warmly, grabbed his arm and dragged him out on the floor, determinedly. They danced the few remaining dances with increasing enthusiasm and warmth. A slow waltz was played towards the end, the lights were dimmed a bit, Bucky knew his stuff. This allowed the dancing to be slowed down, couples to hold each other a bit tighter, and the mood to get more romantic. May and Pat danced that bit closer. They didn't step on each other's toes as they were hardly moving at all, just holding. May loved it. They both felt there was a growing chemistry and affection between them. Neither said anything, just let the magic of the moment carry them.

Then it was over suddenly, the lights went up and Bucky announced The National Anthem. Everyone stood to attention, hands straight by their sides. Most people sang all the words of Amhrán na bhFiann, especially the men, for whom it was an important statement. As all the dancers milled about, looking for friends and moving towards the cloakrooms, Pat put his arms around May and said 'Thank You May, can I see you again if I get in touch, maybe another night dancing or the pictures'? May said 'Yes, I'd love that'. Peter came over to Pat and May saying 'c'mon Pat or we'll miss the last tram'. Just as he was leaving, Pat gave May a peck on the cheek, and off he went with Peter to the door. May floated off to find Rose in the Ladies. As the girls walked home up the avenue, May was still floating on a cloud, but Rose was quieter and a little down. 'I'm not sure about Peter', said Rose', 'he seemed a little less keen tonight than the first time we met, I don't know what I think, and he had a bit too much drink on board for my liking. But don't mind me May, tell us all about Pat'. So May did. Rose was happy for her.

The following day the girls who had 'borrowed' dresses returned them to Ann so they could be returned to the laundry to be put back into the cleaning without anything being known or seen. All that day the girls were chatting away about the dance, and who they danced with. Most were happy but some not so, including Rose. Actually May felt she was one of the happiest after the dance.

Rose and Peter did not see each other again. Peter didn't say why or how he felt. He just said nothing. Pat did get back in touch with May, messages passing through friends of friends. And they did go dancing again, in Blackrock, Dún Laoghaire, and Bray. Their friendship grew and blossomed. May was right, she was in love.

*Pat Swords.
A handsome young man.*

A Bit Romantic
May and Pat   early 1940s

Mae and Pat stayed 'an item' as they said then. Over a period of a few years they drifted into an understanding that they would be married. No engagement as such, no one had the price of a diamond ring, even one reasonably priced from 'The Happy Ring House' in O'Connell Street in Dublin. A bit less than three years after meeting at Bucky Devine's dance in the boy's school , they were married. A low key wedding, not that there was any reason to be low key apart from there being no money for a big 'do'. No Princess wedding dress here but rather a simple stylish suit of jacket and skirt for May. Looking great. Pat wore a goodish dark suit, styled by Burtons, and paid for in Burtons over a great many weeks on 'the never-never', a large white carnation on his lapel. Also looking great. A wedding cake was made, iced and decorated by May's friend Angela who was good at this and had what they called 'a great eye for it', as a wedding gift. The party walked to the church around the corner from the house in the Cottages where May was born and grew up, and May and Pat walked back from the church to the house as a married couple, Mr. and Mrs. Swords. The neighbours all stood out on their front steps to congratulate them and wish them well. In the house loads of sandwiches, sausages, sausage rolls and savouries, nothing too posh, waited for the wedding party. All the close friends were there, some neighbours, some relatives, and Aggie, Molly, Anna and Rose, but no Peter.

The wedding cake sat on the sideboard waiting to be cut and wished over. Lots of carry out from Gleeson's, bottles of Guinness, McCardle's ale, Gin, Jameson and Babycham kept the do flowing along. Someone played an accordion and a singsong started up. Later, a good while later, the cake was cut and shared to well wishes and cheers all round. Soon after, old Mr. Prenter, the nun's driver, parked the car, the nun's station wagon, outside the front door to take the happy couple away. Everyone at the do came out to see them off. The neighbours in the cottages all came out and stood on their well scrubbed granite front steps to wave them off. Other neighbours just twitched their curtains and did not miss a thing. Then they were driven off, covered in confetti, to honeymoon in the countryside. To Rathnew actually, far away in farming countryside, to stay in a cottage vacated by a friend of May's, Annie Doyle, for four days, that's how friends helped each other then, favours given and returned, even where there was little or no money around. May and Pat settled in to a close but meagre married life, but at least they were together and had their home to themselves. Tom, the brother, had moved out and was living in the gate lodge of the convent working for the nuns. Sister Ann had gotten married and lived in one of the new city suburbs, in Islandbridge, then later in Inchicore in a tempestuous marriage, but that's another story. The girls were still good friends, but there was a distance, many were still single girls and May was a married woman, difference and distance were respected. Pat worked at a range of different jobs, one time stoker on an Irish Light's ship with his brother Christy

Swords, like their father, also called Pat, did before them. He also at one time worked for Boland's Mill and Bread Bakery in Ringsend, working night shifts, tough work. At other times he worked for a roofing contractor, Aul' Hammond from Dalkey, in the world of roof tiles, slates, tack rippers and roof lead. He was often away from home for a week at a time, no one had cars to be coming home so they stayed in 'digs', sometimes Pat stayed in little known places like Athy, or Bagenalstown. Away in digs, nights were often spent in a local pub with the lads having the few pints and maybe a game of rings, or playing twenty fives. Pat liked a pint and at home he liked a pint in the bar with the lads, not the lounge, of Gleeson's over the road, or Brady's in Williamstown, or Keoghs in Blackrock. Sometimes he and May went out for a drink, maybe to Gleeson's as it was near, and then into the lounge, that's where you took the wife, but he missed the lads. Pat was not a problem drinker and always made sure to have the few bob housekeeping for May. There might only be a few bob left for him, the price of a few pints and a packet of Players, as reward for a lot of hard work. May got work too, not steady work, but there might be word among the girls of some auld wan in Trimbleston who wanted a bit of cleaning and
ironing done one morning a week, or a retired gentleman in a big house on the Rock Road who needed the place run over and maybe a shirt ironed. It all helped.

*The only picture I have of Pat and May's wedding.
Pat's brother Des, best man, May's sister Ann, bridesmaid.*

A Bit of Disappointment
late 1940s

With any newly married couple then, after a short enough interval friends and neighbours began to wonder if anything was happening. The usual inquiry among themselves, but not directly to May, was often the age-old question, 'er a stir?', to raise the issue in the nicest and most discreet way. For a good while there was 'ne'er a stir', but what only the closest friends like Rose or Molly knew was that there was indeed 'er a stir', three stirs in fact in the first four years of marriage, and all ending quickly in misses. When this situation was investigated with a view to correction, bigger problems were found. Before long May was admitted for surgery and corrective action.

A hysterectomy was mentioned as a possibility. May and Pat were devastated by what they were hearing, and waited worriedly for results and recommendations from the surgeon. The patter of tiny feet in their home seemed remote and far away, most unlikely. They didn't realise then how many years away, another four, or the strange way in which the tiny feet would arrive.

A Bit of News, A Big Bit
Tea in the Burlington   1987

It was late 1987. September I think, or maybe October. I was 37 and married to Jacinta since 1974, with two boys, David, 12 and Mark, 10. We were in the lounge lobby of the Burlington Hotel, large comfy soft seats and low tables, having afternoon tea, coffee and bikkies, Jacinta and I, and Aunt Kathleen.

In my family when I was growing up there were lots of Aunts and Uncles, brothers and sisters who got married and settled down to live not too far away, setting up their own homes, and producing lots of cousins. We were close as an extended family, Aunts, Uncles and cousins and we got together often, trips to Killiney, Bray or Bug Rock for swimming and picnics, trips on Mystery Trains, and all those birthday parties where everyone got together in boisterous celebrations.

Aunt Kathleen was not married, yet she was always at the centre of the fun. She might have been referred to as a 'spinster', but she was too lively, too lovely, friendly and too beautiful a person to be described with such an ugly word. Everyone, in the family and beyond, loved Aunt Kathleen. As all the cousins grew up they all saw lots of her as she visited them all regularly. We all loved her stories which she told and read to us. She would recite poems from memory for us all, poems with moral meanings telling us not to eat string, or cry 'wolf', or tell lies. With Aunt Kathleen, learning was never so much fun.

At special times of the year, Aunt Kathleen would appear to help some of the other Aunts to mix The Christmas Puddings or to prepare, bake and decorate The Christmas Cakes. These were great occasions which all us children loved to be a part of. Aunt Kathleen had the confidence and steady hand to manage the almond icing, the Royal Icing and the tricky art of cake decoration from the mysterious piping bag with all those strange looking nozzles. Us children knew that these special events when we watched Aunt Kathleen work her magic, always had a bonus for us cousins, a hand in the mixing to make a wish, and many spoons and bowls to be licked and scraped before they went into the big sink to be hand washed. Such nights might end with cups of tea and slices of brack for the grownups, with glasses of lemonade and biscuits for the children. These were the type of occasions when if we were lucky we might persuade Aunt Kathleen to recite a favourite tale like 'The Green Eye of the Little Yellow God'. Such stories enchanted us all and carried our imaginations to exotic times and places all over the world and far from our humdrum ordinary lives at home.

We all loved every contact we had with our Aunt Kathleen, such great memories.

All of this when I and the cousins ranged in age from 8 to around 14, and thirty years before the Tea in the Burlington. I grew up in Booterstown with Ma and Da, May and Pat, in Pembroke Cottages off Booterstown Avenue. Aunt Kathleen visited us as often as all the other relatives and cousins, and we all got together often for cousins' birthday parties, and picnic trips to Killiney, or Bray seafront. Eventually Ma and Da and I left Booterstown and moved up to Glasthule to live with Aunt Kathleen in her house, in Findlater Street in Glasthule. Her mother Ellen had died which Aunt Kathleen took very badly, she suffered with her nerves, and she needed the company. She was still unmarried and her house, though small, was bigger than the house in Booterstown, so it made sense to move. I had gone to junior school, a convent school with the Sisters of Mercy only around the corner from Pembroke Cottages. From the age of four I was in Babies and High Babies. I remember a teacher Mrs. Tully, a terror, and a beautiful Nun, Sister Malachy, an angel.

Then to Primary School with the Christian Brothers, in Oatlands in Mount Merrion. A long walk up to school and home, but then in those days of the fifties children walked to school in all weathers and thought nothing of it, there was no one in the family with a car to drive you. I was accompanied for safety by the son of a neighbour, Thomas Long, a few years older than me. So life moved on through Primary School, then into secondary school also in Oatlands College, in the section of the college that was known as 'The Private', though at that time I did not fully understand what that meant or the stress and strain it put on parents to be sending me to a 'quality' school. Good days those in secondary school. This was a time when students got slapped by the Brothers with a leather strap known as 'The Leather'. As I was a bit of a cheeky giddy smart alec, I got slapped with the leather often, and I deserved every slap I got.

After we had moved, Ma and Da and me, to Findlater Street, Glasthule to live in Aunt Kathleen's house in which she had grown up, I continued to attend school in Oatlands College. Most of my classmates were from Stillorgan and Mount Merrion, near to the school. But I was travelling from Glasthule. This involved me walking from Findlater Street along 'The Metals' laneway to catch the number 8 bus to go up the town of Dun Laoghaire to Marine Road, to get another bus, the 46A to Stillorgan and college. The entire two bus process was repeated on the journey home. Often I would walk the first or last leg of the journey, saving some of the busfare which would go towards buying a bag of chips from the chipper, to be enjoyed as I walked along. Most of the friends in school lived near the school, but I and a small few others left after school to go home to another area. It made for a very long day. It also meant that I did not get to mix with school friends outside of school so that even close friends were not as close as they might have been. Also the friends I played with at home had nothing to do with my school life, so there was a disconnect all round. As an 'only child' I was a bit more 'only' than I might have been. I never gave much thought to why this was until long after I had Tea in the Burlington.

Life and times moved on, changing and unknowingly heading towards the Burlington Hotel. For me, school exams, college, work in department stores, in railway stations and then getting a job I wanted in an advertising agency, raced along. Strangely enough I got this job through a regular passenger I got to speak to in Dún Laoghaire Railway Station. Chance and experiences never go to waste. Working in the office in the daytime and studying at night in the College of Commerce Rathmines, I even won The Conlon Gold Medal for Advertising Studies. I was a smart and lucky young man of 22. More study at the Marketing Institute for my degree. Progress at work, promotion, headhunting and getting ahead. Going out with Jacinta since school days. Then marriage at 24 in St Joseph's Church Glasthule, 1974, and a big 'Do' in the Shangri-La Hotel in Bullough Harbour. All the family, cousins, aunts and uncles were at it, it was a great day, Aunt Kathleen was at it, naturally. Changes too in Findlater St. Over the next few years. Ma and Da getting older and more infirm. Aunt Kathleen left to move to Dalkey after the sudden passing of beautiful Aunt Veronica, wife of Aunt Kathleen's brother Des, and mother of young children. Young children needing care and possibly in danger of being sent to an orphanage. Aunt Kathleen volunteered to move there, look after the house, home and children, and keep that family safe and in their own home. It was a marvellous act and commitment on her part, a vocation effectively. It saved the family. Time passed, David and Mark were born, grew, went to school. I was working and concentrating on work too much. Jacinta had worked before we were married, after the children were born, she stayed home to care for the two boys. Aunt Kathleen visited regularly and with Ma - Nana - was a regular for Sunday Dinner while the boys were young. But over the years with the family in Dalkey, Aunt Kathleen was increasingly unwell. She had suffered a few 'turns', or strokes, leading eventually to her being moved into the Royal Hospital,

Donnybrook, not far from the Burlington Hotel. I worked nearby. I had set up my own marketing business, MSA, in Lad Lane just off Leeson Street, Dublin 4. I went regularly to Donnybrook Hospital to see Aunt Kathleen. Sometimes she cried when I arrived, nearly always she cried when I left to go back to work. She was often out of bed and sat in her wheelchair and I could wheel her within the hospital to a canteen for a cup of tea. If the weather was good we went out into the gardens and grounds of the Hospital where she could have a sneaky cigarette. Sometimes I was able to bring her further, down to Donnybrook village for a coffee in one of the pubs. Sometimes we walked towards town to walk down the tow-path of the Grand Canal to see Patrick Kavanagh's Seat, maybe read some of his poems from a book or the poem inscribed on his memorial seat. Aunt Kathleen always loved and recited poetry all her life. I made copies of twelve of her favourite poems, with help from Gráinne who worked with me. We produced and laminated very large copies of the poems with extra large typography so she could read them easily. She loved them. On these walks towards town we would sometimes pass the Burlington Hotel, and I would wheel her in. There were no steps into the hotel, it was easy to wheel her in and around the large spacious lobby. Usually I was alone bringing her there. On this particular occasion Jacinta was with me, we may have all gone on a longer walk, possibly to Grafton Street and we all went into the Burlington on the way back to the Hospital. We wheeled in and organised ourselves in the large lounge onto soft sofas at a low coffee table. We ordered tea, coffees and biscuits and took to chatting. It was always interesting to talk and listen to Aunt Kathleen.

We were always a great family for talking about old times and memories, stories of old or long passed family or relatives, many of whom led colourful and adventurous lives at sea. Aunt Kathleen loved to talk about and remember old times. Out of nowhere I asked her to tell me about Ma and Da and the time I was born, December 1950. I asked her in particular to tell me about Ma's life before I was born. This line of discussion was not planned in advance, it just came up naturally. I asked her to tell us about Ma and Da and me being an only child. I asked if Ma had any medical issues before or after I was born, as in 1950 it was unusual to have only one child, women often had five or six children, or none, if there was any problem.

'Well actually', Aunt Kathleen said, 'Ma didn't have any children at all.

I had the baby, and you're the baby'.

A Bit Stunned at the Tea in the Burlington

'Well actually', Aunt Kathleen said, 'Ma didn't have any children at all.

I had the baby, and you're the baby'.

Stunned silence. And yet a moment of blinding clarity. Everything explained itself, in a flash, the whole relationship, Aunt Kathleen, and Ma, and Da, and me. All the questions I had never asked, if I had known there was anything to ask questions about, but I didn't know, nor ask any questions over the years, there had been no questions I had wanted to ask , apart from the one which I had asked just now and which had opened the door to this dramatic revelation. I looked at Jacinta, and Jacinta looked at me, neither of us knowing what to say.

When I tell this part of the story to friends and family, I describe it as my 'drowning man moment', as if my whole life flashed before me in a split second too small to measure, a million things fell into place, and made sense.

I remember wondering at the time, 'how should I react, should I jump up and throw my arms around Aunt Kathleen and say "Mammy" '. I thought of doing it, but I didn't. I was married to Jacinta with two boys, David and Mark. I felt I could not rewrite nearly forty years of a life I knew nothing about in an instant. I guess I felt I should react like a mature adult and not like a giddy teenager. Compared with the big revelation that Aunt Kathleen was my mother I cannot recall much of what else we talked about. Naturally we asked about my father, my biological father, but Aunt Kathleen didn't want to go there, going only so far as to say 'Let's just say your father was a 'Gentleman' to indicate, I suppose, that he was not a lowlife or ruffian. Perhaps she used the word 'Gentleman' to reassure me that there was nothing untoward or sordid about my conception. She was firmly and steadfastly and determinedly not going into any more detail. She reassured me, and Jacinta, that Ma and Da were still my Mammy and Daddy and that she was still my Aunt Kathleen. She did however charge us with not saying anything more to reveal this news, kept hidden for so long, she explained. She especially did not want us to say anything about this conversation to Ma, or Nana as she was known now, and was called by all the family. I think she was afraid that Nana would be hurt to know that we knew, that it might in some way affect my relationship with her. Nana, all her life had never been good at dealing with anything that involved Sex, Relationships, and Emotional issues, not really having the words and learning to deal with this. Kathleen may also have been afraid that my knowing this story might have somehow seemed to Nana like her taking the child back, even though the child was nearly 38.

I wondered over the years long after both Nana and Kathleen

had passed away that Nana had missed out on her role in the story not being fully acknowledged, after all Ma and Da, Nana and Uncle Pat, were at the very heart of this story.

There may have been other reasons in Aunt Kathleen's mind for not going into more detail at this stage. But it would be many more years and a great deal more information learned before I could begin to imagine some of the complex reasons in Aunt Kathleen's experience as to why she was saying little at this stage. The little bit she was saying was dramatic enough for now.

A Bit of Unexpected Conversation, with Tears and Tea
1987

At home in Beechwood Lawn over the next week or so Jacinta and I discussed this new news , this new development in our lives, and what it all meant. We didn't say anything about it to others, not even telling our sons David and Mark until a few years later. They were still too young and didn't need to know yet. I did however first phone my cousin John in Rosslare. John was like a brother to me and every bit as close to Aunt Kathleen as I was. Our families were very closely linked, John was born in February 1950 the first child of Annie and Jim Goggins. Annie was Kathleen's sister. I was born to Kathleen in December 1950, in fact when I came home from Holles Street Hospital with Kathleen, it was to live with Annie and Jim and John in their flat in the Dun Laoghaire Bridge Club on Corrig Avenue Dun Laoghaire. Kathleen with her new baby was not welcome back into her own home in Findlater Street by her mother Ellen. Actually during Kathleen's pregnancy her mother kept her confined to the house, only letting her out at night, in the dark, to go for a walk so she would not be seen by neighbours. Worrying about what the neighbours would think of such a shaming situation was a great preoccupation in those times. So, John and I were together from a very early age, what I describe as 'Pram Brothers', literally sharing the same pram.

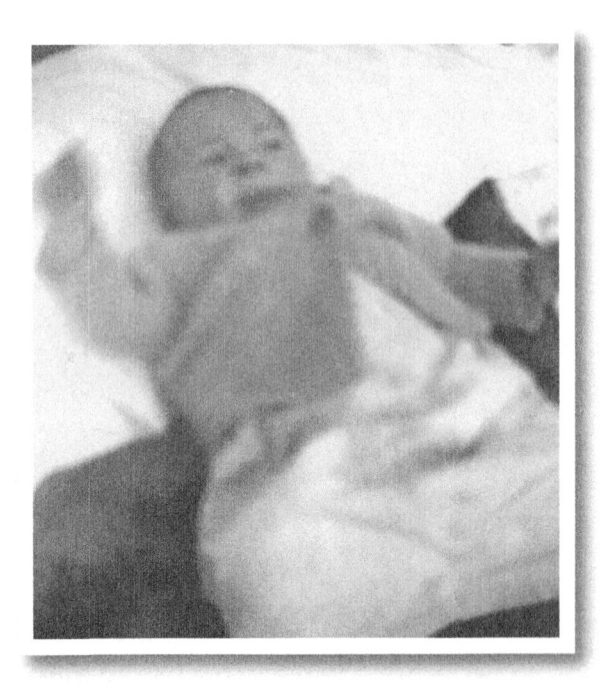

*The earliest picture of me we had in the shoebox.
Aged maybe one or two months, in the pram in the back
garden of 29 Corrig Avenue, Dún Laoghaire.
This was where Annie and Jim took Kathleen and I in.
This was their pram, the one in which John and I were
'pram brothers'.*

So I phoned John to tell him the news. He was as flabbergasted as I had been and like me he found lots of things explained themselves in an instant. I was as amazed as he was that neither he nor I had any inkling of this over the years nor even thought about the family structure to have any suspicions. But why would there be suspicions, everything seemed normal. He grew up in a very normal family situation, mammy, daddy, himself and three sisters and I grew up with a ma and da, an only child. And we both had a lovely Aunt Kathleen. I never thought about it much nor did he, why would we. All the cousins loved Aunt Kathleen and Aunt Kathleen loved them all equally. There had never been any favourites with Aunt Kathleen who loved us all.

Still, Jacinta and I wanted to share this news with somebody, if only to talk it out and help us to understand it better, and to understand what it all meant. We had two very close friends, Paddy and Phyl Lonergan. Phyl had been Philomena Dunne, and as it happened Phyl grew up on Booterstown Avenue around the corner from Pembroke Cottages where I was raised by Ma and Da. Phyl's mother and Ma were close friends. So we phoned them and asked them over for a cup of tea, saying we had something to tell them. We all settled down to tea and cake and I proceeded to tell them about our conversation with Aunt Kathleen. We went through all that was said including the key phrase – 'Well actually', Aunt Kathleen said, 'Ma didn't have any children at all.

I had the baby, and you're the baby'. – the same phrase that Aunt Kathleen had floored us with. It was a very emotional chat over tea and we all were quite upset. I was bawling crying while telling it and Jacinta was bawling crying with me. Paddy was crying while he was listening and Phyl was really crying as the story unfolded.

Except that we were not all crying at the same thing. Phyl was crying for a different reason to the rest of us.

"But Martin, I'm delighted to hear that you now know this. I have to tell you now that I have always known this, that Kathleen was your mother. When I grew up in Booterstown with my Mammy being such close friends with May, your mother, we all knew that you were Kathleen's Child. Sure when I was small I used to wheel you in your pram, around the Cottages and into the church grounds. We all knew but it was not something I could tell you or talk to you about until now, until I knew that you knew yourself. More tea and more tears, tears of happiness.

In discussions with other family members and a wider family circle of relations I discovered that they all knew about Kathleen's child. But they all also understood the code of secrecy, that things like this within a family were not for discussion or spreading around. It was over. It was in the past. Leave it there. It would have killed any of them if they had been the first one to tell me this truth of my birth, if I had not already known, and they didn't know if I knew because they wouldn't

*Group of close friends from Booterstown on an outing by train.
Left, Elizabeth Dunne, Phyl's Mother. Centre, Kathleen, then May,
then Nana Blake, Phyl's Grandmother.*

ask me. It would have dishonored Kathleen and the family if they had been the one person who told something that was not supposed to be told. Until Kathleen told me herself, I was almost the last to know.

As this new news settled in with Jacinta and I we began to realise that many relationships which had been taken for granted might now need to be reappraised. For example with my relations and especially with my cousins. May's sister, Anne, who we all knew as 'Granny Ann', had married Jack Cardiff and lived in Inchicore. Their children Paddy, Ann - who we knew as 'Young Anne', Elizabeth, known as 'Beth', and Deirdre, known as 'Deirde' or 'Dee' and their youngest son John had always been my cousins, but were they now that May was not my birth mother, were her relations still my relations? What did it all mean? May's Brothers John and Willie had families who were all my cousin's, same thing. For me at age 37 with a family of my own, I felt I could not reorganize my past life and their past lives and start thinking of them all differently. I decided to leave well enough alone. I had grown up with all this family of cousins and they were, and always would be my cousins, I could not rewrite my past and their pasts. We were all and would continue to be 'Family'. The same issues did not arise on the Swords side of the family as Kathleen and Pat were brother and sister. The children of their brothers and sisters, Annie, Des and Christy Swords were all still directly my cousins.

To go back to John, my pram brother and closest friend, and

*The Mammies and the Aunts at a
swimming trip to Bug Rock.*

*Typical 'Cousins' day swimming at Bug Rock.
John Goggins and Paddy Cardiff, top. Angela Goggins, Beth Cardiff,
Deirdre Cardiff, Mary Goggins, Me, John Cardiff, Susan Goggins,
centre and front right. Great fun.*

the fact that neither of us had any inkling or suspicion of this relationship with our Aunt Kathleen, I did recall a conversation I had with John when we were around 13 or 14. At the top of Findlater Street where I lived in Aunt Kathleen's house, number 19, with Ma and Da and Aunt Kathleen, across the road there was a place called The Bank. Climbing a five or six foot wall got you up onto The Bank which was full of smallish trees and bushes, elders and such like, and we would play up there a lot just climbing the trees and hanging out, being brave. At the top of The Bank was a broken wire fence and beyond that you looked down into the steep cutting where the railway ran carrying the trains from Bray to Dublin. So it was a dangerous enough place to be, no wonder we weren't supposed to play on The Bank.

I recalled that conversation I had with John though I don't know what led up to it. I told John that I didn't understand my relationship with my mother, May. I felt I didn't love her as I should. I felt that she didn't seem to me to be very maternal in her relationship with me. I didn't know what it meant or why. I didn't say that I felt closer to Kathleen because I didn't, she was just lovely Aunt Kathleen to me, to John, and all the cousins. Nor did I give any thought at the time to being an only child and not having brothers and sisters like all the other cousins including John himself. I didn't really know what I was thinking or feeling, just that I felt I didn't love my mother May in a way I should, and I didn't know why. I didn't know what brought on this line of thinking and talking or why I was talking it out with John. John had nothing to say by way of an answer or advice, and I wasn't expecting any. I was just thinking out loud I guess. We were both too young and the subject was beyond us. I didn't know then what brought up this line of thinking and talking. But now I'm glad I said it and that we both remember it being said. There must have been something hidden deep in my unconscious mind that triggered it. And why John? Who else would I be able to say such things to when you're only 13 or 14.

Over the coming years when John and I together were researching our family history painstakingly, and sometimes painfully, I was glad we had had and recalled this shared conversation as we pieced the story together. This conversation was like an anchor in our search reminding us both that some vague feelings occurred underscoring all that we learned later. I was glad it was John that shared and confirmed these thoughts. Over many years later when I was exploring and researching this story with family, friends, and colleagues of Kathleen's, I often deliberately brought John with me to assist me in these meetings as by this time John had become the genealogist of the family and 'keeper of the records'. It was also to help me remember what was said and discussed, as I began not to trust myself to remember what was said, and what was the chemistry of some meetings. Just like the conversation on The Bank.

Two to remember.

*On a walk on Booterstown Avenue,
being taken out by May's good friend Angela Byrne.
Love the coat.*

A Bit Complicated Being Born Again.
1988

All of this newly discovered news was happening towards the end of 1987, getting on for Christmas. Christmas had to be prepared for, and enjoyed. Where possible we had in the past tended to host Christmas. Jacinta and I and the boys, we nearly always had close relatives, family and sometimes friends join us for Christmas. On many occasions I would collect Ma and bring her up to our home. I also on many occasions drove into the Royal Hospital in Donnybrook to collect Aunt Kathleen and bring her to our house for Christmas, complete with wheelchair so we could all have Christmas dinner together. It was difficult and awkward but it was always worth all the trouble. It was great to see Ma and Kathleen enjoying what was a nearly normal Christmas, just like in the old days. I don't know what the boys made of it all, but they were good about it, good on the day and helped with the washing up. We were aware there might not be many more Christmases like this but we didn't mention it, just thought about it.

We didn't mention the new and dramatic news though it was on our minds constantly. We just got on with life and all we were doing. Apart from this new knowledge everything was the same as it was before we knew. We were determined however that we would have to find out more about this story. But where to start?

A birth certificate, that would be a good place to start. We dug out the old box of certificates, marriage info and all the family photos and papers. I knew I had a Birth Certificate because I had needed one for school, confirmation and for getting married. And there it was, my Birth Certificate. But it was the short version of my Birth Certificate, and apart from a few dates and my name, it told us virtually nothing else, no parents or other details. Then it dawned on me that this was the only Birth Certificate that I had or had ever seen for all these years and occasions. I had never seen or been shown my official long-form birth certificate for all of the almost 40 years of my life. There were also boxes of many old family photographs, mostly in black and white, many of me as a very small baby or as a toddler, many more of family outings, picnics, and trips to the seaside with the extended family, parents, in-laws, cousins, aunts and uncles. Our own two children from an early age with parents and grandparents. And always Aunt Kathleen. These photographs would have to be assessed and re-examined very carefully, but not today, not yet, first we needed to get a copy of my Long Form Birth Certificate.

In early January 1988 Jacinta and I were at the counter in the public office of the Registrar of Births Deaths and Marriages near Westland Row in Dublin city. When our number was called we approached the officer at the counter. We explained what we were looking for, giving our names, dates and address where I lived when I was born. The officer asked us to sit and

wait, saying he would call us when he was ready. He was gone a long time, a very long time. I was about to get up and go back up to the counter when I saw him. He was at the door leading from the public area into the back offices. He was not alone. He was with an older lady, probably a Supervisor. They were talking and looking at the public waiting outside. I got the feeling he was pointing us out to the Supervisor, presumably talking about my inquiry. Then they both went back into the back office. After a little while he came back to the counter and called us up. He explained that most of the requests he dealt with were very straightforward, others were more complicated. My request was complicated, he said. I didn't understand.
He assured me that they had found my information, but asked us to go with him to a private room as they needed to talk to me and ask some questions, and preferably not at the public counter. We followed him into a meeting room where there was a Supervisor waiting for us, the lady we had seen him talking to. They sat us down and he proceeded to talk to us before he showed us anything. He asked me a lot of questions. I realised much later that he was trying to establish how much I knew about my birth and childhood. This I suppose so that whatever he was about to divulge did not completely shock or upset me, though he did not explain it in those terms.

I explained that I knew my birthday, the ninth of December 1950, and about growing up being reared by my mother and father May and Pat Swords in 7 Pembroke Cottages

Booterstown. Also that we moved house around 1959 to 19 Findlater Street Glasthule to live there with Aunt Kathleen whose home this was. I also explained to him the news that we had learnt just recently from Aunt Kathleen, that she was in fact my real mother, my birth mother, and that I grew up being reared by Ma and Da, May and Pat Swords, and that Pat Swords was Aunt Kathleen's brother. The Supervisor said nothing but took a lot of notes. The officer asked all the questions and took his own notes. In the beginning of the interview there was a tension in the room but the more I explained the little I knew, I could sense the tension lighten in the room, I could see the Supervisor and the officer looking at each other, there was even the odd smile.

As it turned out his news was more dramatic than I could have imagined and yes it did shock and upset us, bringing on tears of surprise, tears of happiness, and yet more questions to be mulled over.

He explained that unusually I had two Birth Certificates. The first showed my birth in Holles Street Hospital on December 9th 1950.

The Birth Certificate showed me as born to Kathleen Burke, married to Thomas Burke, labourer, at the address 29 Corrig Avenue, Dun Laoghaire. And amazingly my name was not Martin Swords but Martin Mary Burke. This was all staggering

news to Jacinta and myself.
But there was more.

The second Birth Certificate produced in 1954 showed different information. There were a lot of notes on the revised Birth Certificate of 1954 correcting the names to Kathleen Swords, unmarried, eliminating all references to Thomas Burke, labourer, and the Corrig Avenue address, showing the address now as
19 Findlater Street Glasthule.
And I, the baby, was named Martin Mary Swords.
But there was still more.

I wasn't actually asked in the interview if I knew I was adopted, but it seems I was. Towards the end of the interview a final Certificate was produced, a Certificate of Adoption dated 1954 showing me formally adopted by Mary and Patrick Swords of 7 Pembroke Cottages Booterstown. It was just as well I had demonstrated in the interview how much information I knew. If I had not known, and all this landed on me out of the blue, I would have been in bits.

We could see then what the Officer and the Supervisor were doing in assessing how much we knew, otherwise this whole event could have been traumatic for them as well as for us making the enquiries. No doubt ours were not the first, nor the last such dramatic discussions in these offices in the Register of Births, Deaths and Marriages.

Original Incorrect Birth Certificate.

These are the amendments required to be made to the original Birth Certificate.

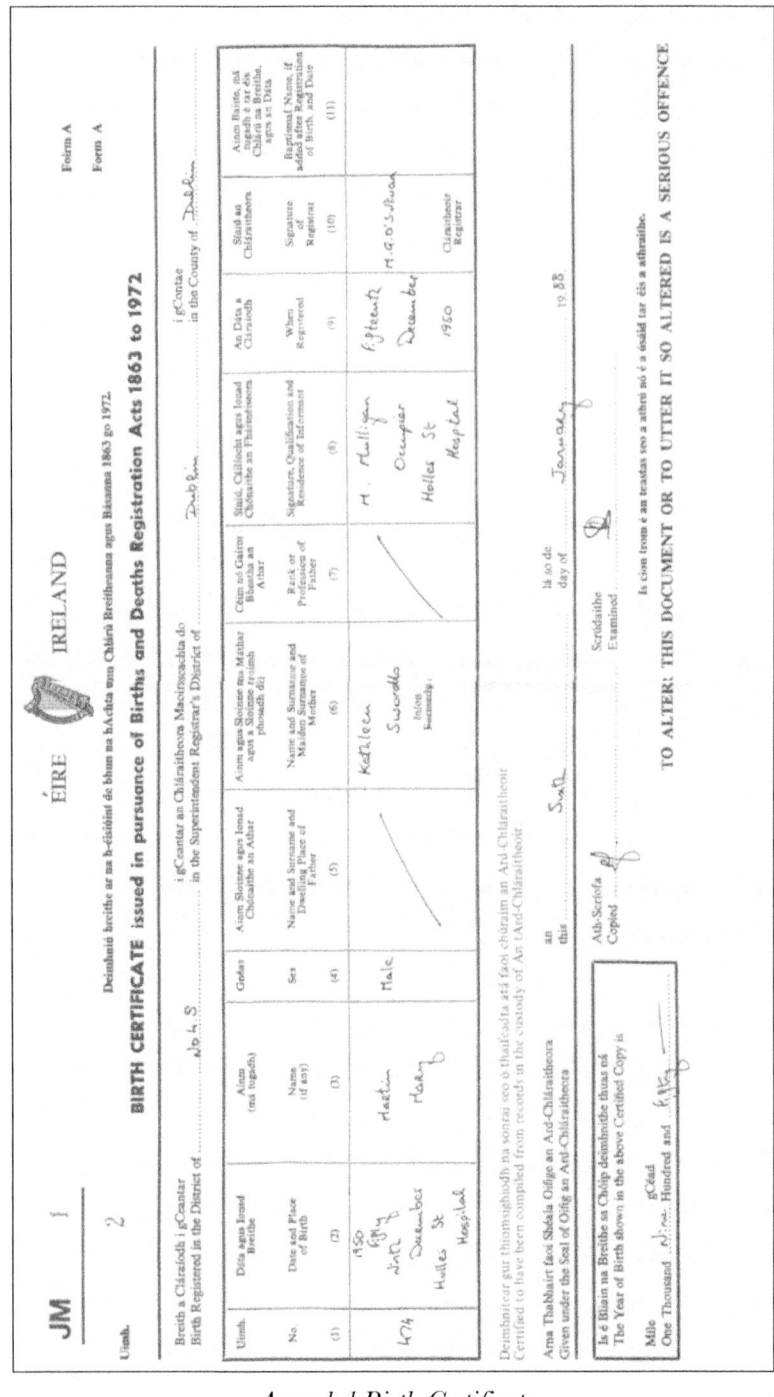

Amended Birth Certificate

Certificate of Adoption

The interview ended, all smiles and handshakes and drying of tears. We were given the printed copies of the certificates all dated the sixth of January 1988. The officer left and wished us well. The Supervisor stayed on with us probably to put us at our ease, to talk and to explain a few things to us. She explained that everything we had learned was not unusual for births from around that time and earlier, less so for later years. She explained that the gathering of birth information at that time was often quite casual, after the birth, the information was often compiled by a nurse going round from mother to mother asking for the details, name ? married? Father's name and occupation? address? baby's full name? Whatever the nurse was told was accepted, there was no requirement to produce a marriage certificate or other proof, many birth certificates were compiled with false information particularly in respect of marriage details to give the baby the best chance by having a 'normal' Birth Certificate, and to avoid the stigma of being the baby of an unmarried mother. Also, as most of the maternity hospitals were run wholly or in part by nuns from religious orders the question might arise, should the baby be taken home at all by an unsuitable unmarried mother or arranged to be taken to an orphanage from where "with God's help the baby might be adopted into a good Catholic family and raised as a Catholic". So, for many mothers it was best to tell lies.

The supervisor went on to also explain that the reason for the amendments and reissue of the second birth certificate in 1954 was to facilitate the adoption. At the time I was born in

December 1950 there were no legal adoption regulations in Ireland. The supervisor explained that prior to adoption legislation in many situations where children were born to unmarried mothers informal adoption solutions were often found quietly within extended families, many of these informal solutions worked very well and were never formalized in later years, even after legislation. Many Irish babies born and raised by grandparents went on to discover many years later that the person they knew as their older sister, was actually their mother.

However when adoption was legalised in 1953 it became the legal situation that a baby could not be adopted where both parents were still living, or if one parent was deceased, that would have to be confirmed by provision of a Death Certificate, in this case impossible as the named father had never existed. So Kathleen had to amend the original Birth Certificate by sworn affidavit, changing the names and removing references to a husband and a marriage, none of which were real, and had been made up by her, albeit for good reasons, to allow the informal adoption to be formalised.

There were still a few questions to be answered such as the fictitious choice of address, details of the baby's life between birth and the informal adoption almost one year later and the circumstances and terms if any, for the formal adoption in 1954. It would take a good many years before these and other answers would emerge from detailed searches, and a few lucky breaks.

This is the famous photo of me aged two which was kept in the family shoebox of old photos for as long as I can remember. I still have one of my blond curls from then which was a common practice. It's in an envelope in a jewelry box, not a shoebox, alongside a silvery ponytail of mine which I grew during the covid lockdown of '20/'21, when we could not get haircuts, and during which same lockdown I wrote this Memoir to keep myself sane.

Family folklore has it that when this photo was being taken in the studio, I did a wee wee on the photographer's cushion, causing those who brought me there, probably May and Kathleen, to beat a hasty retreat - Morto !

A Bit Frightening in the Storm
1956

I guess I was around 6 years old or maybe 7 when this thunderstorm story occured. I was living at home in 7 Pembroke Cottages off Booterstown Avenue living with my Ma and Da who had adopted me, though I would not know anything about this for another 30 years. Anyway I was at home mostly with Ma, Mary Swords because Da, Pat Swords, would be away at work.

Ma had a couple of little jobs cleaning and ironing for families, or for single gentlemen in the general Booterstown Blackrock area. Most of the mammies in Pembroke Cottages had little jobs, and word was always circulating among the wives of new jobs, a man living on his own who needed someone to 'do' for him, cleaning and ironing of a Thursday morning say. When Ma had to go on a little job she would often bring me with her, I being an only child and no one to babysit me.

I went to some strange places with Ma on her little jobs. One I remember was to Rathmines, a good bit away by bus and walk, by what I guess was called Shank's Mare. It was in an upstairs room above a shop in Rathmines Main Street, to clean what was called a 'Pongo' room. Pongo was a game which predated Bingo. The room was laid out in a square with seats for players on raised platforms around the room. In the centre was a large wooden box with sloped sides leaning inwards towards a wooden grid of upright boxes, into which the players threw a cloth ball they were given. The wooden spacers where the ball settled were numbered and the caller would call out the number where the ball landed. Players, mostly women, marked their cards with a marker, calling out 'Pongo' when they had filled a line or a panel. The numbers were checked and verified, and prizes awarded. The games were held at night, and the players drank and smoked furiously all night. Ma's little job was to clean up the following morning with me in tow. The place absolutely stank of beer and cigarettes, bottles were scattered and ashtrays were overflowing with ash and butts and sweet wrappers. It was a horror, even to me who didn't help at all, but played at throwing the balls into the Pongo box.

Not all the times I went with Ma when she was cleaning, were happy times. There was a house in Mount Merrion where she cleaned which was a less than happy experience for me but Ma knew nothing about it. The house was at a crossroads, not far from Trees Road. It was a corner house with what seemed to me a large side and back garden, there was a wooden garden shed in the back garden, and it was in that garden shed that I was sexually abused by one of the sons in the family. The woman who employed Ma was a nice woman, raising her family in a modern house, yet she seemed hassled and nervy, not as nice and happy as some of the other ladies who employed Ma. I don't remember how many children were in the family, but I clearly remember the two teenage sons, they might have been around sixteen. Anyway one of the teenage sons took me into the garden shed where he abused me, playing and touching me and making me play with and touch him. I had no idea what was going on, I was six, but I just felt it was not right the few times it happened. A frightening part was the son's insistence that I say nothing or tell no one about it, I didn't, I was too afraid to. Looking back it seems to me that the boy's stern warning not to tell anyone or say anything about it was more frightening to my young mind, than was the touching, which I didn't understand. It's strange that this has stayed vividly with me all my life. I remember the house and the family's names. I walked past the house on a visit to Mount Merrion many years later. The shed is still in the back garden. Maybe all the well off happy homes in Mount Merrion were not really happy homes at all.

There were a few other places Ma brought me to, but the best by far was to Mrs. Finn's house on South Hill Avenue, between Booterstown Avenue and Mount Merrion Avenue. The Finns were a well-off family and I got to play with the Finn children's toys when there with Ma. They had a toy car big enough to sit in, with two pedals which you pushed back and forth to make the car move forward. I had never seen the like before and I loved it. But even better than that, the Finn's had a television with a small screen in a fancy wooden cabinet that showed a black and white picture. I didn't know how to put it on but sometimes it was left on for me. On the small screen a fuzzy crackly picture in black and white showed the BBC children's programmes in the afternoon. My favourite was Torchy the Battery Boy, an early puppet animation. To this day I can still sing the opening song, 'Torchy Torchy the Battery Boy, he's a Walkie Talkie Toy' . Other favourite programs included Noggin the Nog and Ivor the Engine. I watched these programmes, glued to the TV set while Ma did the hoovering and the ironing for the Finns, whose house I didn't want to leave.

So what has all this to do with a storm? My cousin, Ann Cardiff, known as 'Young Ann', the daughter of Ma's sister Ann, known later as 'Granny Ann', was often staying in our house in Booterstown. Ma minded her a lot from the age of 2 due to some upset in Ann's home. Ma's sister Ann had married Jack Cardiff when she was still under eighteen, and they had lived in Islandbridge, and later in Inchicore. It was not always a happy house and young Ann loved staying with Ma, her Nana, in Booterstown.

As she was older than me she sometimes minded me if Ma was out at work, and Anne and I were in the house alone on this occasion, when the storm started. We heard it nearby, and getting louder as it got nearer. We were on our own in the house and terrified. Ann, being older, started to do the things she had learnt to do from other adults when in a thunderstorm, even though she was terrified and trying to be brave for my sake. We pulled the curtains, and with towels and sheets we covered all the mirrors. We also covered the large pictures in glass frames, the picture of the 'Big fella', Michael Collins, the picture of the 'Long fella', De Valera, the picture of Pope Pius XII, and the picture of the Sacred Heart of Jesus. Most houses had these same pictures, and they were covered because it was believed the lightning would flash into the house and bounce around from mirror to mirror, or from picture to picture and strike you dead wherever you were in the house. Even small mirrors on dressing tables were covered. The lights and electricity were turned off in case lightning shot through the electric wires outside and inside the house, burning out the wires and the fuses, and starting a fire in the wiring. While we were doing this the storm was getting bigger, louder, faster and nearer. We knew we had heard something about counting the seconds between the Flash and the Thunder to see how far away the storm was. This knowledge was no good to us, there was no gap of seconds to count. The Flash and the Thunder were together at the same time. Did this mean that the storm was directly over us? We could hear the lightning crackle, we could hear the thunder rip instead of roll. We could feel the air and the house shake with the thunder. This storm was so near it must have been only a few feet above the chimney on the roof. And for the first time ever, and the last time since, we could smell the lightning, a strange strong smell like water for washing the clothes in. We were really terrified to experience this massive storm so closely. And no sign of Ma coming home. Ann and I pulled the sofa out from the wall and hunkered down behind it, pulling a hairy blanket over the two of us. Strangely neither of us noticed that there was no rain falling in the storm but we didn't remark on this until much later. We were too busy saying our prayers under the blanket, like we had seen the adults doing before. We started a few different prayers, we got the first line or two of most but couldn't go on, we had forgotten the words. Before the storm was over Ma came back from work, coming in the back gate and the back door, well shaken and also terrified, having walked home during the storm. We were glad she was here to take charge but she was so shocked with the storm that she was as bad as the two of us. She just got behind the sofa with us and joined us under the hairy blanket, at least she knew the prayers, so we prayed.

Eventually after a long time the storm diminished or passed away. It took a long time for us and the neighbours to get back to normal, to get over it. No one seemed keen to explain how they had hidden, and how afraid they really were. OK they all spoke of covering the mirrors and all agreed that that was the right thing to do. None of them, including us, admitted to getting down behind the sofa in terror. But many of them remarked on the strange smell from the lightning, which all agreed was the strangest thing ever and probably came from some Divine intervention, someone suggested fire and brimstone, whatever that was. There seemed to be little or no real knowledge of thunder and lightning and how they really worked. But later in a friendly folksy way it was explained to us in child friendly ways. It was Giants throwing boulders at one another up in the clouds. It was herds of Heavenly red-eyed cattle stampeding on the Heavenly Plains. The one I liked and could relate to as an Irish explanation, was that the thunder was the sound of Angel Brewers rolling barrels in Heaven and they bashing into each other making crashing thunderous noises.

Years later I thought what a strange thing to tell a child about a storm, about porter barrels and men working with beer, and yet in the 1950s working class families would be very familiar with pubs, and with beer and barrels. We had all seen the breweries delivering barrels to the pubs, rolling them off the truck and dropping them onto straw filled cushions on the pavement, and from there they were rolled, rolling them noisily on the path to the big open trap door and dropped into the cellar to land on an even bigger straw filled cushion with more thundering noise. Many of the barrels were still wooden casks although the new all metal barrels, called Firkins, were starting to be used.

So that was the story behind Thunder -'Thunder Barrels', and what could be a more friendly and reasonable explanation for an everyday weather occurrence. And a very useful and necessary explanation, sure if there was no thunderous banging of heavenly barrels, in heaven or here on earth, there might be no beer, and what would we all do then, they said.

A Bit of a Near Thing Around the Corner
1956

I have no great recollection of being in any rough trouble involving fighting when I was this age. I suppose I was a good boy. There were all the usual scrapes and falls while quite young playing in Pembroke Cottages and attending St Mary's Infant School, the school around the corner on Rosemount Place. Badly scraped knees while scuttin' on the back of the Johnston Mooney and O'Brien horse-drawn bread cart. I slipped whilst scuttin' on the back of the cart, got caught up and dragged along, fortunately being horse-drawn the bread cart was not moving too fast, but I had very bad scrapes, with small stones and bits of tar embedded in the wound. I got lots of TLC from the neighbouring Mammies as they cleaned the wounds using scissors to take out the small stones, dressed with plenty of Savlon ointment and some other pink stuff, and lashings of Vaseline to top it off. I got a whopper of a bandage that any young boy would be proud to wear as a trophy, and a limp for about a week. I was very brave, so they said.

Kenny's Field was another matter altogether though. Behind our house in The Cottages was a field known as Kenny's Field, it was a sloping field with bits and pieces of rusty farm equipment such as pronged rakes and harrows from when Kenny's did a bit of farming locally. Kennys had had a small dairy yard nearby, and even kept a few cows in the field from time to time. It was a great field for us youngsters to play in, rusting farm machinery and all, to climb over and sit on the shiny metal seats, pretending we were farmers or cowboys. But there was a pit in the field. Quite a deep pit with straight sides and water and mud at the bottom. It was dangerous, you'd know just to look at it, which made it very attractive to play around and throw stones into. In the pit was growing an assortment of briars, thistles and stinging nettles, all the nettles of the world were in there growing vigorously. Which is where I fell in. Playing too close to the steep edge I slipped into most of the nettles and thorns. When you're wearing shorts there is nothing that nettles like better than a virgin leg. The other lads gathered round and looked in, glad it wasn't them in the pit. Using a few rotten planks of wood found around the field, and lads holding other lads by the legs and using jumpers and gansies I was reached and pulled slowly from the pit. Wherever I had exposed skin, I was stung and that included arms, neck and face. I could tell where it hurt, in all the places where it swelled in red lumps. I was bundled by the lads around the corner to my home. Once again a host of 'Nurse' Mammies among the neighbours attended to me. I was stripped and slathered with lots of stuff I didn't recognise, but mostly I think, stuff called Calamine Lotion, they all swore by that. And Vaseline again, everywhere. I was given a few junior aspirin and put to bed with hot milk to make me sleep. No talk of doctors or driving to A&E then, you did what you could with what you knew, some of the Mammies from the Cottages had worked in a hospital, possibly in the kitchen or canteen once, but they knew stuff. The stinging pains went on for a few days but the red weals and lumps took longer. I was a hero for a while but I didn't want to be a hero.

After the stinging episode, and while I was still suffering, something came along to distract me from my woes. The Rag Man came calling to the cottages and streets around. Sitting up on his horse-drawn flat cart the Rag Man did not have to announce his arrival. The children's grapevine went into overdrive and all the children rushed to gather up old clothes, and some not so old, to give to the ragman in exchange for toy trinkets. We rushed about the house getting old clothes no longer needed to make up a sackful. Sometimes the Mammies knew what could be given away from worn out clothes. Sometimes older clothes were grabbed anyway unbeknownst to the Mammies, and stuffed into the bag. Sometimes clothes for the Rag Man were simply found. On a derelict empty house on Rosemount Terrace, an old old lady called Biddy had once lived in squalor. She was gone now, possibly dead, but her squalid rooms were raided for torn clothes, shawls or shoes for the Rag Man. And all for what? The toy trinkets were worthless but we wanted them. Cheap wooden soldiers or toy whistles, bamboo whistles, which when you blew into them inflated a balloon, then as the balloon emptied the air back through the bamboo whistle it made a long drawn-out whistling screech. All good rubbishy stuff, like what you'd get in a Christmas Cracker, only better. The Rag Man didn't check the clothes too closely, he was too busy loading up and dispensing goodies, and being careful his trinkets we're not being stolen by eager thieving hands in the chaotic exchanges, but I suppose he knew what he was doing. We never questioned it or thought about why he was collecting rags for trinkets or what happened next. For us it was stuff for nothing and that was great. He only called to the streets about twice in a year, so he created a frenzy of excitement when he visited each time. Years later someone told me the Rag Man took the rags to the Rag Mill at the Paper Mill in Islandbridge. I hope he made a few bob out of us, and I hope he looked after the horse. I doubt it.

This was fine and childish while I was attending the Junior School of St Mary's Convent run by the nuns of the Sisters of Mercy. I would be leaving soon and going to the big boys school, Primary School in Oatlands in Mount Merrion. But before I left the convent school there were two events of note in my memory. We had a mix of nuns and lay teachers in the convent school. One, was lovely, kind and full of goodness, Sister Malachi, whom I always remember from that old questionable practice in all the convents, collecting a 'Penny for the Black Babies'. We all had to bring in our penny every week for the collection box to help fund the nun's missionary work in educating children in Africa. We were constantly being told how lucky we were here in Ireland with Mammys and Daddies and good schools to learn in, and to pity the poor children of Africa who had nothing, at all at all.

Prince Charming and Snow White. That's me as the prince, look at the costume! and Sheena O'Donovan as the beautiful Snow White.

Another teacher, not a nun, was Mrs Tully, a dragon of a woman who was always cross and intimidating. If you were sent to Mrs Tully you were in trouble. I was sent sometimes.

A school play was being put on, part of which was a small piece of the story of Snow White. A lovely sweet girl called Sheena O'Donovan from down on Booterstown Avenue, beside The Punchbowl, was Snow White, who had to be asleep at the end of the scene as the Wicked Queen had cast a 'sleeping spell' on her because she was too beautiful. I only had to appear briefly, no speaking part, to be Prince Charming, who would arrive and administer love's first sweet kiss to the sleeping Princess thus breaking the spell and reviving her. That's all I had to do, say nothing, just kiss the Princess. But I got a lot of ribbing from classmates over the kiss. 'Ooooh's and Yeuch's' and 'How Could You' and such like, usually from the boys, the girls said nothing other than 'The Princess was Lovely'. The play was a great success. But I especially remember well the hectic activity at home with the making of my Prince costume. Long wide trousers, shiny shirt, a big heavy cloak, and bandana style hat worn as they say on the Kildare side. Best of all worn in my wide belt, a big plastic sword like a Pirate or a Prince would wear.

The convent school was literally 'the school around the corner' from Pembroke Cottages. There was a famous programme on Radio Eireann called 'the school around the corner', presented by a famous broadcaster and ex-teacher called Paddy Crosbie.

He visited schools and interviewed the young children asking them to talk about school, to sing a song or tell the listeners a 'funny incident', either a joke or unusual story. Being live radio, not everything went to plan. One famous 'funny incident' told by a hard chaw in a city school told of a horse pulling a cart, falling into a roadworks excavation. The young lad told of how seriously the horse was injured and how it had to be put down in front of horrified onlookers. Paddy made the mistake of asking the young lad if they shot the horse in the head to which he replied 'No Sir, they shot him in the hole'. Poor Paddy didn't know what to say or where to look and nearly choked trying not to laugh. There was quite a bit of an uproar over it from those who thought it rude and unsuitable.

Well it was announced in St. Mary's convent school that in about a week Paddy Crosbie himself would be coming to our school, to make a program of the school around the corner for RTE Radio. For about a week we had to learn and practice the theme song for the programme.

" Oh the school around the corner's just the same
The school that taught us how to play the game.
It hasn't changed at all
The old table's in the hall
Oh.... the school around the corner's just the same."

We didn't need to work too hard to learn the song as we already knew it well. We all loved and listened to the programme on the radio. We were all told to think of things we might say or funny incidents to tell if we were picked to be on the programme. Four of us in the class, including me, were told quietly to have a really funny incident. The four of us were confident and outgoing pupils and good talkers. As the time grew closer we were all excited, animated and nervous. Two days before Paddy Crosbie was due to come to our school I got sick with a very sore throat. On the day he arrived I was worse with laryngitis and had no voice at all. I was in bed all day so sick I didn't care about what I was missing. I would not be back in school for two days and a weekend. Two of the pupils got on the programme, they sang songs and one of them told a funny incident about his granny cooking an apple tart sprinkled with salt instead of sugar. The tart was awful. So was the story.

A Bit of Growing Up During Some School Days
1960

The move from the convent school run by the Nuns to Primary School in Oatlands run by the Christian Brothers was a big move. Leaving childish things the move was into older more grown-up lessons and behaviour. The Brothers were very different to the Nuns and set about establishing the ground rules very early. Basically you do this or that the way we tell you to do it. If you don't you will be punished, slapped with the leather, then you will do as you're told and we'll all be very happy ok? It didn't take long and not too many slaps to get the message. Over the next few years we got it, and got sorted into our class streams. Not everyone was bright or top of the class, not everyone was so bold or difficult to handle that they couldn't be sorted out. Classes were streamed into best (A), middling (B), and the rest (C), so that those best able to, could make progress at a pace. I was never top streamed but I was a happy and contented 'B'. Students who fell behind or struggled were usually (C)s, but still learning at their own pace. Some who dropped out or just disappeared from roll call tended to be (C)s, when they left they weren't looked for too hard. I was smart enough but not always smart at my lessons, just smart in a smart alec witty way, so I was popular.

Not all the teachers were Christian Brothers, there were many lay teachers also in primary, but men, always men. The closed mindset of Ireland in the 1950s and 60s was not yet ready for women teachers in a Catholic boys school.

One memorable teacher we had was a Mr McGreil. he was tall, thin and had oily hair too long swept back with a very high forehead. His skin on his face was tight and taut as if it was rubber stretched too tight on his head. He had a wide mouth with a prominent full set of teeth many of which were discoloured and bad, a dominant feature. The teeth and skin gave him a look of a skull, unforgettable. But it was his mannerisms that were most intriguing. His physical appearance and way of moving his hands was very theatrical. You might have said he was a bit of a luvvy but we didn't know that word then. You might also have said camp, gay, queer, or even effeminate and affected, but we didn't know these words or descriptions either, so we just thought him odd. Still, for all that his classes were often interesting especially when he wandered off the subject he was supposed to be teaching. Mind you he wasn't beyond imposing discipline with a few slaps of the leather when required, even if he had to do a bit of a twirl as he slapped your hand. All the teachers used the leather, especially the religious Christian Brothers. It was just the norm, nothing special. I was smart, confident and what might be known as a bit of a messer. I would often be more interested in whispering or cracking a joke with some of the lads in class, having a laugh, rather than paying attention. I got slapped with the leather often enough, sometimes it was seen as a badge of honour. We usually got four, two on each hand, occasionally six for a bigger offence. I got six sometimes. You could see that the Brothers put their backs into it and the slaps were not just casual or easy but strenuous wallops. I don't know if they enjoyed giving the leather but some of them gave it a lot too much. And it hurt like hell, especially the third one on each hand that had already gotten two . It was important to stay stoic getting the leather, not to cry or cry out in pain. A steady unshowing stance was required, a defiant 'I don't mind' stare that stared down the Brother giving out the slapping was required. You sat back down unflinching, but your hands really hurt, they were numb and stung for a long long time. Blowing on them, or sticking them into your armpits didn't really help. You were too sore to laugh and too afraid to cry even if you wanted to. You were somehow being brave for the other lads and defiantly silent. Not easy.

Looking back on school from much later in life, and hearing horror stories of sexual abuse of boys by Christian Brothers I know it happened and was widespread, although it didn't happen to me, nor did I see it happen. It seems as though abusers and groomers avoided boys who were confident, outgoing and likely to stand up and speak out. The boys more likely to be targeted were timid, controllable and suggestable, of which there were many in school with me. The question of abuse was not widely discussed or commented on by us boys, we didn't have the knowledge or vocabulary to deal with the subject. But it was widely known and commented among us that there was one particular Brother, involved in the area of science, who was to be avoided, especially when students were alone. We would not have had the right words like 'paedophile' at the time, but 'fiddler' would have told us what we needed to know.

I had a few close friends and we tended to hang out together during lunch breaks. Jimmy Doyle from Stillorgan and Jack Brennan from Bray, Billy Saunderson from Cabinteely, and me from Dun Laoghaire. As we all went our separate ways after school we never met outside of school to share our social activity. When we sat together with friends in the school yard and all talked innocently I heard a phrase that stayed with me all my life. Someone would say 'tell us a picture', meaning tell us about a film they had seen in the cinema. We all loved going to the pictures or 'flicks'. Often the film we told about was a cowboy often known then as a 'horse opera'. Telling the story often took us back into the world of 'The Chap'. The Chap was the clean cut guy in the white hat, who though often put upon, saves the town from the Baddies. The Bad guys in the black hats always needed a shave and were given to chawin' tobacco and spitting on the street. Our world and interests then were very innocent.

Being an Irish Christian Brothers school great emphasis was put on sport which was encouraged for its good character building and good living qualities. And being an Irish school, Irish sports were emphasized. Good clean honest rough tough Gaelic

Football and Hurling as played by Our Fathers and Forefathers, and others before us, who had died for Ireland, good clean Irish Catholic games. Not for this school deviant foreign games like soccer, too English, or aristocratic upper class rugby, too Brit, too public school. No, the games the Patriots of Ireland played were the games for us boys, (there's a lot of good Catholic Irish Ethos tied up in this way of thinking). There were other famous boys schools not too far away, run by different religious orders who excelled at games like rugby – 'West Brits the lot of them' – not said out loud but thought and understood nevertheless.

Anyway, I hated sports.

Being a popular character in class I was always picked when it came to picking teams for Gaelic Football. Never picked first mind you, nor second third fourth fifth, usually around 6 or 7. But never last, I was never left with the tail end hopeless cases who had no chance of ever touching the ball once during the game. I was popular; it would have been insulting to leave me to last. But I probably should have been left. The two guys who were real good footballers got to do the picking. After they picked those they knew who could run fast and read the game, they picked from the rest in equal measure. They knew I couldn't play well but on the off chance I would stumble on a stray ball or manage to trip an opponent and his way to scoring, I was in. Most games, I was far out on the wings kicking the mud with my boot, moving a worm cast and wondering how many worms there might be in the piece of earth under my feet down to a depth of two or three feet. It would be interesting to know that. Meanwhile, from my lonely station far out on the wing I could hear and see the noisy melee in front of the goal mouth move as one from side to side, to be followed by a loud roar as our side scored a goal. Oh well. I never understood or cared how the good players, who only seconds ago were standing at their own goal mouth, yet seconds later were positioned perfectly in the opposition goal mouth in precisely the right place to jump, catch, dribble, kick, and score the goal that made our team roar in celebration. I was in awe of their ability to read the game. What was the score? I'm sure we must be winning by now. Whatever about the sacred patriotic association between this game and our historical, political, cultural, and religious heritage, I was unmoved.

As for hurling, that was just terrifying, savage. No thanks.

Yet all was not completely lost however. For some inexplicable reason I was involved in a worthwhile fashion with the school's athletics activity. I achieved a passing long jump, but I could not master the triple jump at all. Nor the high jump. In the high jump world at the time the hot new thing was the Fosbury Flop, a style of jump that to my eyes looked illogical, unnatural, and defied the laws of both gravity and common sense. I walked away from that. Yet I was found to have a good arm for throwing the javelin and the discus. Probably as these were activities suited to a solo 'only child' individual kind of application, utilising weight, mass, and strength of arm (one), I seemed to have had something to offer, rather than in team sports. I did actually represent the school in interschool sports for the javelin and the discus. However the opposition fielded a team of Goliaths to our little group of Davids. We never won.

So much for sport, what about lessons.

Three good friends at Oatlands.
Jimmy Doyle, left, Martin, Jack Brennan, right.

*At my Confirmation in Oatlands.
Kathleen, proud as punch.*

A Bit Better at Some School Lessons
early 1960's

So, you see, at school, sport was not my finest hour. Come to think of it, lessons and academic subjects were not my finest hour either. I was never top of the class, never a pupil that excelled at tests or exams either. But I was never the worst, somewhere in the middle, or I'd like to think just above the middle, just above average, but never the best. The streaming system meant that the really bright boys and those with an aptitude for say mathematics, forged ahead in some disciplines, and this I think was a good thing. They needed to be stretched in their abilities and some of the Maths Heads soon exceeded the requirements of the curriculum or even the abilities of their teachers. Most of us however were happy in our 'B-Stream World' to get by and be comfortable in our abilities. Getting by often meant being able to keep up with the expected standard and to be happy. A few students struggled and fell behind the pace even in the B-stream. Falling behind and struggling was not a good thing and became very stressful for some students. There was usually no coming back, not easily at least.

My level of comfort and ability for different subjects was really dependent on whether or not I found a particular subject interesting. Interesting subjects for me included History and Geography. Physics I found interesting, but not chemistry. Physics I could see, but not Chemistry. Mathematics was not interesting for me at all, and I never got it. Maths was further complicated during my time by the introduction of 'New Maths'. 'Old Maths' often involved what might be known as 'hard sums', but new maths took us into the world of calculus, algorithms, sines, tans and new concepts that were effectively a whole new language of Mathematics, I was getting lost. Other languages I struggled with included French and Irish, more on this. But the subject I loved and did very well at was English and English literature. I see now 60 years later that the world is divided between 'word people' and 'numbers people', perhaps that is why at over 70 I still love a crossword but have no time or talent for Sudoku. I can't see the point.

So, of the subjects I found interesting, Geography and History were among my favorites, I think because I could relate to them so easily. Geography was all around me, at home we often went out as a family, to the hills and countryside on family trips, to beaches, forests, hills and rivers where we talked about what we saw. Our family was always interested in interesting stuff, assisted by our regular visits to the Carnegie Library at the far end of the town of Dun Laoghaire, with Pat and Aunt Kathleen. I found I was learning stuff everywhere, not only in school. On our forest picnics I could show you and explain a 'meandering' river almost before I could spell the word. Similarly with history, the subject was interesting because at home we often talked about olden times, knights, mediaeval life, monasteries and ghosts, heroes of Irish history and a million failed Irish rebellions. We often heard talk at home about an older relative or a neighbour whose father had met and fought with, say Michael Collins or Dan Breen, and have the photograph to prove it. History was just outside on the street, if you asked the older neighbours who remembered the 'Black and Tans' banging all the front doors, including ours, with their rifle butts. What I loved in history was the story element of it rather than the details such as dates. Sometimes my interest in English got mixed up with my approach to History. I recall writing an essay exercise about the battles at Vinegar Hill in Enniscorthy, my story opened with the line 'Dinny, do you think will we ever get out of here alive at all', the teacher thought it was a great story as he returned our work a few days later, 'great story' he said, 'but a few dates and details would be a good thing in a History exercise, don't you think?

Religion was another subject in which I was distracted by the story rather than the dogma. As a teenager I was questioning everything inwardly, and, like many other students, we were afraid to question what we were being taught. The Christian Brothers teaching us did not take kindly to independent thinking – 'just accept, learn and memorize what the Church is teaching you'. Again I was more interested in the physicality of Bible Stories and the context in which the story occurred - 'how far was it from Bethlehem to Jerusalem, and how long would it take you to walk it' What did the plain people of the Bible eat?, it can't all have been loaves and fishes, and how did they cook it'. I was inclined towards religion class more as Archaeology rather than Theology, Dogma or Blind Faith. Then there were all these other exotic and interesting World Religions. No one in the Christian Brothers was telling us anything about these. I do remember thinking in class, 'there's all these other religions, they can't all be right, they can't all be wrong. What makes ours absolutely right and the others absolutely wrong. Questions like this were not up for discussion in the Christian Brothers. Maybe they were all wrong, including ours. I was afraid to ask. I just didn't get it. I still don't.

French was another interesting subject, class was taught by a lovely teacher, a Mr. Heeran, tall, elegant, reddish hair, he was a Gentleman who's classes we all found very interesting. I recall, as with all the other languages we did, that there was a great deal of emphasis on grammar and writing the language. Not nearly enough on the spoken language. We never learnt how to chat up a girl at a dance, in French. Or how to order a round of drinks or a meal in a French bar or restaurant. We never discussed a headline from a French newspaper, that might have been helpful, but then this was all way before the internet, and we lived very insular lives. However the best thing about Mr Heeran's French class was that he could easily be distracted away from the lesson during the class. There might be a question from someone prompted by an Irish news headline, or some news story in International Affairs heard on the radio, and a fascinating discussion would ensue, fuelled by more questions and observations from all of us students, enough hopefully to stretch the discussion to the end of class, and never get back to the French. I learnt more about Civics, Politics and Human Nature during those discussions in French class. I met Mr Heeran many years later at a school reunion and I remarked how much we enjoyed those free-ranging discussions whenever we managed to cleverly distract him from the French subject. 'But you didn't distract me from the lesson' he said, 'I distracted you. Those discussions were very interesting and most enjoyable, I deliberately kept them going, even to the end of class. I'm glad you enjoyed them. There's more to life than French grammar'. Good one Frenchie.

Now, Irish class was something else. Irish was taught to us with a patriotic passion. To not like Irish, or to not be enthusiastic about learning Irish in class, was almost an act of treason in our newly emerging independent Ireland. We were forced to learn Irish because it was regarded as a 'badge of Irishness', sacred to our Irish identity and necessary to preserve and revive our native language, so long suppressed and outlawed in our troubled history of occupation over 800 years. So, saving the Irish language by teaching it in schools was mixed up with Religion, Catholicism, and the patriotic fervor of our forefathers who had died for Ireland. And all we had to do was learn our own language. We were even incentivized further to learn Irish, if we choose to do some subjects in our Leaving Certificate, things like Chemistry or Physics, through Irish rather than English, we were awarded extra marks in our results for doing this. Presuming of course you knew Irish well enough to understand Chemistry and Physics in Irish, when many of us struggled to understand Chemistry and Physics in English.

The learning of Irish was pushed down on us very hard. As a result we hated it, and struggled with it badly. Two or three generations of students through the '40s, 50s, and 60s, hated Irish and were turned away from it, quite the opposite result from that intended by the civil servants and the Department of Education.

I have no real memory of Irish lessons being pitched around real life and the use of spoken Irish, how to pay a bill in Irish, how to buy a bicycle in Irish, how to talk to a girl while walking along the road in Irish. Instead the emphasis was put on grammar and writing, reading, and memorizing Irish poetry which we did not understand. How many students of Irish, like me, continue to be haunted by the Tuiseal Ginideach, the genitive or possessive case of words in Irish, which was made so important in the teaching of Irish Grammar. We were never encouraged to love Irish outside of a patriotic nationalist context. Generations have experienced this and many are only coming round in older age to want to learn to speak the Irish language with pride, after all we are Irish.

Strangely it took me years after leaving school to realise that the teaching of modern Irish history, Irish Catholicism, and the passionate teaching of the Irish Language were all inextricably linked. The modern Irish history we were taught at school ended at 1916 on the steps of the GPO in Dublin. We didn't deal with World War One, The Great War, we didn't deal with the Anglo Irish War, or the Irish Civil War. We were a very young independent country and the traumas of those Wars, and of the Anglo-Irish Treaty were very fresh and recent to us in the 1940s, 1950s and 1960s. Memories from these traumas were perpetuated down to my time in school, teachers did not teach or discuss these traumatic events, possibly because their own parents, relatives or friends had been active participants in these conflicts, on all sides of the conflict, and may have been victims or perpetrators of conflict and violence. It was all too recent and too traumatic. The recent family ancestors of students and the recent family ancestors of the teachers may well have fought on opposing sides of the Irish Civil War. Into this delicate mix the role of religion and religious orders such as the Christian Brothers, played a part, the passionate teaching of Irish became in a sense an expression of patriotism for whichever side of the modern conflict your views have come down from. There were many clerics and religious on both sides of modern Irish conflicts, involved in actions both heroic and treacherous. For the Christian Brothers teaching us Irish with passion, they must have felt that God was on their side.

So my experience of learning Irish in school was poor, ranging from awful to not good at all. and yet for all that it seems that

I remember the day this photograph was taken in class for a Chriatian Brothers archive. Naturally we were all told not to look at the camera and to look natural. But when did I ever do what I was told to do. That's me at the back window, chewing my pencil and looking quite cool if I say so myself. Brother O'Sullivan was taking an Irish class. Some of the boys in this class went on to be famous; some in the class have passed away. It took me years of searching to find this picture.

more than a few words and phrases in Irish learnt at school are not forgotten and come back to mind much later in life. Our Leaving Cert Irish had penetrated more than we realised. My cousin John who was always good at Irish went on much later in life to take Irish classes in Glencolumbkille in Donegal and is now a fluent speaker of Irish. Even in banter with him I will throw in a word or phrase of Irish that I didn't realise I knew or recalled. Indeed many Irish people who would say they cannot speak Irish have like me a bit more Irish than they are aware of. I guess we should thank the Christian brothers for this but not for the harsh way they went about teaching it. How much better they would have done in the long run if they had taught us to love the language and not to fear it. Could they not see this at the time or was their enthusiasm clouded with passion and patriotic fervour.

*Mr. Padraig Heeran, - 'Frenchie' - a very popular and very effective teacher.
I have no recollection of him using The Leather or any physical punishment, a 'Gentleman'.
Pictured here at a 40th Past Pupils reunion with Dermot Aughney and Billy Saunderson.*

A Bit Better at English Class

The subject I liked best in Oatlands primary and secondary school was English and English literature. I was good at it and felt for it. Because I liked it, it was not difficult and therefore seemed easier, because I was enthusiastic about it. It was easier to be good at something you liked rather than a subject you struggled with. Chemistry it was not.

Because I liked English I had read the texts, prose poetry and Shakespearean plays very early in the year from cover to cover, over and over ahead of the pace of the English curriculum. Even material not on the syllabus I had read and enjoyed. In addition I had my own reading interests at home. The Beezer, The Dandy and The Beano I loved. Also Marvel Comics from America and exciting Superhero characters like Green Lantern and The Hulk. Why do I remember from the Hotspur and the Victor, all my life, the stories of the Jellymen and Alf Tupper when I have forgotten my Chemistry formulas. In addition to Comics there was my own reading from the Dun Laoghaire Library, The Carnegie, where I was an enthusiastic borrower, with Aunt Kathleen bringing me and encouraging me. I love going to the library to this day, and still recall the dry dusty and musty atmosphere there then. The place was always hot and dry with large storage heaters too hot to sit on or stand against while browsing. Mostly all the books were dull and uninviting looking, cloth and cardboard covers with names on the spine. No colour covers or dust jackets. Books were arranged in sections like biographies etc. I like to borrow from the section on travel and exploration so I was reading early about travel up the Orinoco, Kon Tiki expeditions in the Pacific, or Easter Island Moai statues. To read about young men in Papua New Guinea and their initiation ceremonies of throwing themselves off high trees, tied on their ankles with strong lianas, to swing bungee-like only inches from the ground was heady stuff indeed for a young boy in Glasthule. Being an only child in a house full of adults was a big factor too. I read a lot at home and lost myself easily in books from the Library or School, in a house that encouraged reading. All were reasons perhaps why I loved English at school.

My English prose book was well thumbed, with stories by R.L. Stephenson, Brendan Behan, Ben Kiely, James Plunkett, Liam O'Flaherty, Seán O'Faolán, and among the very few Irish women writers in the book, Mary Lavin was outstanding. Excerpts from Somerset Maughan I loved, but then I was reading his books at home outside of school as well. A particular story which intrigued me was 'A Dissertation on Roast Pig', by Charles Lamb. An intriguing absurd story of the discovery of Roast Pig following the accidental burning down of a pigsty in China and the subsequent tasting of Roast Pig. This discovery was followed by a manic campaign of burning down buildings containing pigs, just to produce Roast Pig.

The madness of the story is that no one stopped to think about it, that there must be a better way. Eventually they did figure it out, but the original story highlighted the frailty of human thinking.

English Poetry was a vital part of English class in secondary school. I read the course book eagerly but I have to admit I struggled with much of it. We studied all the classic poets, Keats, Byron, Shelley, Hopkins, and I have to say I did not like most of them, no matter how famous they were. I found the language to be strange and old-fashioned and whatever they were setting out to say, they seemed to say it in a very ornamental and flowery way. I didn't speak like that, and knew no one who did, so they didn't draw me in. I loved the sheer strangeness of William Blake and loved his 'Jerusalem'. I also loved Coleridge's 'The Rime of the Ancient Mariner', even though the language was archaic, yet the story and dramatic context held my interest. It was the sheer storytelling of it that I loved, it was such an unusual Morality Tale. Many of the other classic poets I found too flowery, I wasn't sure what was being said and I did not like how it was being said, even with our own National Poets like WB Yeats.

There was however a dramatic turnaround starting with the poem 'The Listeners' by Walter de la Mare. This poem held my attention and took my breath away. It was a story being told to me, but what was the story? The poem never fully explained itself and left the imagining of the story, including the before and the after to the reader, which I loved. Also the language used and it's poetic constructs were like the language I used myself. I was hooked. This poem caused me to explore a lot of other poetry, and took me to Owens, Sassoon, Frost, Kavanagh, and Heaney. I revisited Keats, Byron, and Shelley, but didn't change my mind about them. I left them alone, there was so much more to discover. I completed my Secondary schooling with the Leaving Certificate. The only Honours level I took and was awarded was Honours English. I was happy with that. I went on later in life to work in Creative Communications, and also to write my own poetry and short stories, forever in debt to Walter de la Mare and The Listeners.

The Listeners

BY WALTER DE LA MARE

'Is there anybody there?' said the Traveller,
   Knocking on the moonlit door;
And his horse in the silence champed the grasses
   Of the forest's ferny floor:
And a bird flew up out of the turret,
   Above the Traveller's head:
And he smote upon the door again a second time;
   'Is there anybody there?' he said.
But no one descended to the Traveller;
   No head from the leaf-fringed sill
Leaned over and looked into his grey eyes,
   Where he stood perplexed and still.
But only a host of phantom listeners
   That dwelt in the lone house then
Stood listening in the quiet of the moonlight
   To that voice from the world of men:
Stood thronging the faint moonbeams on the dark stair,
   That goes down to the empty hall,
Hearkening in an air stirred and shaken
   By the lonely Traveller's call.
And he felt in his heart their strangeness,
   Their stillness answering his cry,
While his horse moved, cropping the dark turf,
   'Neath the starred and leafy sky;

For he suddenly smote on the door, even
   Louder, and lifted his head:—
'Tell them I came, and no one answered,
   That I kept my word,' he said.
Never the least stir made the listeners,
   Though every word he spake
Fell echoing through the shadowiness of the still house
   From the one man left awake:
Ay, they heard his foot upon the stirrup,
   And the sound of iron on stone,
And how the silence surged softly backward,
   When the plunging hoofs were gone.

Source: The Collected Poems of Walter de la Mare (1979)

A Bit of a Fight
1958 ish

During my time in primary school at Oatlands I don't remember very much in the way of physical confrontation among the boys. There was all the usual jeering, pushing, chasing, catching someone and pinching them or pulling their hair as boys do. But there wasn't any big stuff, no scraps as such. There was however one scrap I remember well, because I was in it.

Most of the lads in the class were around the same build, some a little taller and thinner, some a little shorter, but none of us was huge, what you might call a bruiser. I was average or just below average in height and build. At around 11, hormones make a mockery of averages. There was however one boy in another class in the same year who blew the averages out the window. His name was Noel, and I cannot recall his surname. I seem to remember Noel came from Donnybrook direction, and Noel was a bruiser. Where we were average size for ten or eleven year olds, Noel was huge. Although he was around the same age as us, Noel was built like a 16-year old, tall, broad, and heavy, he towered over us all. A Giant to all our little Pixies playing in the yard. Noel was big, but he didn't have what you might call a big personality. I knew of Noel, everyone did, you couldn't miss him, although he mixed with his own friends, he and I didn't mix or talk, we were in different groups. I on the other hand had a personality, not for stature or for strength, but for being a bit of a lad, a cheeky chap with a witty remark or answer. I wasn't a leader or anything like it but I was 'well known'. Maybe Noel knew me, I don't know. I was known as 'Swordsy' then, but Noel's friends knew me I'm sure. And my friends knew Noel and his size and presence. We were like two planets in orbit in the schoolyard, both attracted and repulsed by each other. Nothing was ever said directly from one to the other face-to-face, but there was a growing inevitability that the orbits would collide. This was not arranged in any way by Noel, or by me. But it seems that Noel's friends had decided there was only room for one planet in the schoolyard. Again nothing was said face to face, but it was whispered by Noel's friends that Swordsy had said something less than flattering about Noel, and he should know. My friends said nothing to me but I'm sure they were making up their own lies as to what Noel may have said or thought towards me, and my friends were aggrieved and put out on my behalf, whether I wanted to be put out or not. Sooner or later in the schoolyard, in the melee of boys, with an air of excited anticipation in the air, a crowd formed a circle, and Noel and Swordsy were pushed into it and into one another, amid calls of 'Fight, Fight' ringing out, while things that were supposedly said by each party were being shouted by each camp. Being pushed together in this arena, engagement was unavoidable and commenced, there being a certain amount of 'face' to be saved. No punches thrown, a form of stand-up wrestling ensued. Noel was huge and I could not get my arms around him to any effect. He on the other hand could push his hands down on my shoulders or on the top of my head, and he did. He could easily lift me up, which he did shortly in a giant bear hug which lifted me off my feet, and with no feet on the ground, I was being shaken like a rag doll. This upright situation did not last long, we both fell clumsily to the ground, me more clumsily than him, as the circle in the yard tightened and the cries of 'Fight, Fight' increased. There was a good deal of flailing about to no effect and I knew that my good school trousers were going to be torn or dirtied, the things you think of at the most inopportune of times. In any case Noel had me on the ground on my back and succeeded in sitting on my chest in such a way that I could see straight up his nose. I was going nowhere. There were no flying punches, kicks, broken noses, split lips or teeth knocked out, just someone sitting heavily on someone else's chest, and the someone being sat on, not being able to move at all. So we stayed amidst the shouts until one of the lay teachers broke into the circle, dragged us both upright and forced us to shake hands. For Noel it must have been like shaking a doll's tiny hand. It was just as well it wasn't one of the Christian Brothers who separated us, or we both would have gotten the leather. There was no blood spilt, it was probably a more innocent time, pre internet, pre video and pre graphic violence. We both went off with our respective friends, tails between legs, if we'd had tails, or at least mine was. Noel was not dragging his tail as he was being clumsily carried by his friends and followers, not exactly a shoulder high lap of honour, he was too heavy for his friends to lift that high. No more was said. Nor was there any return, those who felt this ought to happen had had their day and Noel had obviously won. I tried to work out that it was a draw, but I couldn't convince myself. Clutching at straws.

I don't know where fate led Noel later in life, I think he may have left school early. I doubt very much if Noel will ever read this but if he was to read it, Good Luck Noel !

A Good Bit of Music
1963/4

At school in Oatlands or indeed anywhere else, I couldn't sing to save my life. Not a note.

There was a great tradition in the school of putting on an Operetta, Gilbert and Sullivan. This was driven by the music teacher Mr Murtagh who managed the whole project from start to finish. The process started with Mr Murtagh calling the auditions. There was no escape, Mr Murtagh insisted that everybody was auditioned, on the off chance that some talent, unknown even to the singer, might emerge. The audition began, we were all lined up and each in turn asked to sing a few notes. My audition was brief and lasted all of one and half notes, followed quickly by that well known phrase from the world of music – next! I was devastated and disappointed. I never expected to be in any prominent role in the production, a non-singing spear carrier perhaps would have done, or a voice hidden, lost in the chorus of other voices, but no. There was no room on Mr Murtagh's stage for anyone who couldn't sing, even in a crowd. So my starry career as a singer in Oatlands never got off the ground.

But I was still interested in music if not in school then at home, among family and relations. If I couldn't sing neither could I play a musical instrument, to my continuing shame. The type of music I was exposed to in the family often appeared at parties at home or in relatives' houses. The old type of party where guests were expected to have a party piece to play or sing or even to recite. The 'noble call' where a performer had the right to call someone at the party to do the next turn applied. And then when the noble call went out some who feigned shyness were reluctant to play or perform, but they always did after much persuasion, which they craved. Others who fancied themselves as singers would be highly insulted not to be called. But their form was always well known, and they were called, even if they were left hanging till late. Some singers had egos bigger than their range. There might be a piano in the room to help start up a sing-song, or to delicately accompany a singer. When someone was singing the hushed room paid rapt attention and respect to the singer. The singer often put himself at the centre of attention by standing at the fireplace, one hand leaning on the mantelpiece and the other hand holding a glass of Jameson. The singers got respect even if they had to demand and arrange the respect they needed themselves. The songs I heard at parties like this or on the radio were older songs popular in the 30s and 40s - Rambling Rose, Red Sails in the Sunset, or even The Pub With No Beer. This kind of music at home was self-made entertainment with no gramophones or records involved and all pre television. The arrival of TV killed off a lot of this 'at home' entertainment. Where music was played at a 'do' in the house it was often Irish traditional jigs and reels, with Irish dancing if possible. I recall rooms being emptied of furniture with only a few chairs for musicians on such occasions. John's father Jim was an accomplished fiddle player, playing often at the Comhaltas Ceoltóri Eireann sessions in Monkstown. On one memorable occasion our relation Richard Coleman was home visiting from America and a really big music night was organised for the whole family to celebrate Richard and his wife Maisy. It was too big an event to hold at home and so it was held in the Workman's Club in Dún Laoghaire, the crowd ran to 70 or 80 and it was a great night. We still have the photographs to prove it. I liked listening to Jim playing the fiddle and as a younger boy I had his heart broken constantly asking him to play 'The King of the Fairies' for me. He never refused. So, a lot of the music I was exposed to at home was fairly traditional and conservative. but we were teenagers and we wanted our own music.

Not all of the good stuff we learned, the stuff that stayed with me all my life, was learned in class from a teacher in school. A huge part of my music interest for all my life came from a fellow student and had nothing to do with the curriculum. I met and befriended a classmate – Johnny Norris. Johnny was a musician, a guitarist even then, and he knew his music well. He was from Mount Merrion from a well-known famous family and was a family relation of Senator David Norris. When Johnny and I were friends in school we discussed a common interest in music, American Folk and Blues music. Johnny introduced me to the likes of Woody Guthrie, Leadbelly, Sonny Terry and Brownie

*The gathering for the music session in The Workman's Club,
Dún Laoghaire celebrating the visit of Richard and Maisy Coleman
in 1960.*

McGhee, Lightning Hopkins, Dave Van Ronk, and Ramblin' Jack Elliot, by lending me some of his LPS. Importantly, Johnny loaned me a copy of a set of LPS called The Folk Box, a set of six LPS which presented the world of American Folk music with sections on European and African roots, Irish and Scottish Sources, Delta Blues, Protest Songs, Work Songs and many more. It was a fabulous set of music. No one at home in my house would have been interested in my interest in this type of music, but John and Angela, my cousins, would be. I took the set up to John's house in Sallynoggin and we played, studied and loved the whole box which set us all up for life with an interest in Folk Music.

But most important of all Johnny Norris introduced me to Bob Dylan who was like a breath of fresh air in all our lives. A lot of the music we encountered before Bob Dylan were crooners and mooners-in-juners, safe music. Even Lonnie Donergan and his Rock Island Line was still a bit polished with Lonnie singing in his dress suit and bow tie. Bob Dylan by comparison was dangerous and revolutionary in the world of folk, protest, even rock and roll. I bought Freewheelin and Bringing it all Back Home in Murray's record shop in Dun Laoghaire where the young dangerous music was sold, and where the young dangerous young men smoked reefers in the dark and dangerous coffee bar downstairs. Myself and John and Angela played them all night, studied and analysed the words and music, and still were confused. But we loved them even if we did not fully understand them, they were our kind of music, and the times were indeed changing.

Of course we also followed The Beatles, The Kinks, and The Rolling Stones, all new music out of the UK. The only similar event to our discovery of Bob Dylan was our discovery of The Beatles release of Sgt Pepper's Lonely Hearts Club Band, the 'must have' album of its day. Again I bought the LP in Murrays of Dun Laoghaire, and again John and Angela and I played it to death and analysed it to death for all its hidden meanings and dangerous brilliance.

I lost touch with Johnny after leaving school but I see he went on to be a prominent performer and a famous teacher and publisher of discs and texts on guitar playing. Thank you Johnny Norris, I have stayed with Folk, Blues and Bob Dylan all my life and I even find myself now here at 70 writing this on the weekend of May 24, listening with the world in celebrating Bob Dylan's 80th birthday.

Somehow not making it through Mr Murtagh's operetta audition doesn't seem so bad from this distance given all the variety of music that I have learned and loved.

Johnny Norris, Classmate and friend at Oatlands.
Thanks Johnny for the music, for American Folk and Blues and for Bob Dylan.
Martin.

A Bit Unexpected
October 1951

Is the baby coming? Really, is the baby coming soon? Ann Cardiff was asking all the questions of May and Pat. Yes, the baby's coming uncle Pat told Ann. Ann Cardiff, young Ann, had been living in Booterstown for a while now, and over recent years on and off. Her home was in Dublin in Inchicore with her mother Ann, Granny Ann, and her father, Jack Cardiff. But she spent time living out with Mary, Nana, as there was often a troublesome atmosphere in Inchicore because of Jack, and drink, and tempers.

At the time Ann was staying in Booterstown, until things worked out, herself and May, her nana, had been busy cleaning and preparing a room and cot for the new baby coming. Clothes, blankets, pillows to be washed, aired and fluffed up in anticipation. The room may have been painted and freshened with the windows opened wide for air. There may have been a little teddy bear sitting on the pillow waiting.

Is the baby coming soon? When? Ann was asking Nana and uncle Pat. Soon she was told. Tomorrow.

The next day was all excitement. Too exciting for breakfast, for shopping, or for any of the ordinary daily chores. No, this was a special day. It would require a lot of waiting. During the morning Aunt Kathleen arrived, there were cups of tea to be had, and hushed whispered conversations, most of which Ann did not hear properly, or possibly Ann was not meant to hear, or would not have understood anyway. After the tea and the chat, Aunt Kathleen left with Uncle Pat and said they would be back as soon as they could, and to keep the fire on and the place warm. Will they bring the baby then, Ann thought, but was afraid to ask. Nana was fussing and fustering all day, keeping busy. Ann could not tell if Nana was happy or sad, or both. Ann caught her crying sometimes.

Around the middle of the afternoon, after Ann had been looking out of the window a hundred times, she heard the key turning in the front door lock. Nana opened the door and there stood uncle Pat and Aunt Kathleen, and in her arms she was holding the baby, me. There was a great fuss and a lot of cooing.

Years later when we were both adults and going back over family history Ann told me this story. It's such a happy day for everyone concerned, with the baby coming home. May or Nana, Pat or uncle Pat, Aunt Kathleen, and Ann, and me. Everyone was happy cooing and ogling the baby. Ann was delighted too that the baby had come home at last, but for Ann something was not right about the happy day. Even at such a young age Ann knew that babies were very small when they were born and brought home, yet even big babies were not this big. When I was brought in I was a very big baby indeed, because I was 10 months old. It was that long since I had been born in Holles Street Hospital in December 1950. Naturally Ann thought the baby was being brought home from the hospital as a newborn baby, and she was shocked at how big I was. As she said later when she told me this story, I nearly walked into the house. But then what Ann didn't know at the time was that I was being brought home by Aunt Kathleen and uncle Pat, not from the hospital, but from Temple Hill Orphanage in Blackrock, run by St. Patrick's Guild. This was in October 1951 and I had been in the Orphanage since April 1951.

*Da, Pat, in the back of
7 Pembroke Cottages, Booterstown,
with Me aged around two, and
young Ann Cardiff.
Touch of the Pioneers in the Wild
West about this scene.*

That's a bit better looking.

A Bit Late for Kathleen
August 1994

It was a Thursday morning, the 19th of August in 1994, when the call came. I was in the office of my own business, MSA, in Lad Lane working with Gráinne. The office in Lad Lane near Leeson Street Bridge was not far from Donnybrook Hospital where aunt Kathleen was hospitalized. It was close enough so that I often got the chance to run in and visit her during lunch time if I wasn't away on an appointment or with a client. Aunt Kathleen had been in Donnybrook Hospital nursing home for some years and while she had her ups and downs over the years there were more downs than ups over the last year. After her earlier strokes and failings we could all see she was poorly, and more so as time passed, she was not picking up.

So when the call came from Donnybrook Hospital looking for me I was surprised yet not surprised. The lady, a nurse or matron I presume, said that Kathleen was poorly and that I should try to come that day. There was no alarm or urgency in the message, I was not told to rush or that the situation was terminally bad. I got my briefcase and stuff together and told Grainne what was happening and that I possibly might not get back to the office, that she could man the fort and head off when it suited her. I left to get my car and headed over to Donnybrook Hospital. On the way there I was passing by a design consultant where I got design work and artwork done when required. I had with me in the briefcase some copy and a picture reference for a design job that was ongoing at the time. So I stopped at the design consultants and left the material in with John who ran the place. John was having a coffee as ever, so I had a coffee with him while I briefed him on the new material. 10-minutes. Then I headed on to Donnybrook Hospital, parked the car and walked into the building with its many long corridors and into Kathleen's ward. 10-minutes.

I saw her in her bed on the right hand side lying sleeping on two pillows, her hair uncombed and hanging in front of her shoulders, arms out over the blanket just as I had seen her sleeping peacefully many times before. Except that she wasn't sleeping, this time, she had just passed away, she was still warm. As I was beside her holding her warm hand and kissing her warm forehead and sweeping her warm hair off her face the nurse came over to me and to Kathleen. The nurse seemed as surprised as me that Kathleen had passed away, however much they might have expected it, but not quite yet. The nurse explained that Kathleen had just fallen asleep, as she had been doing regularly that day and recent days. It was as if the nurse, like me, expected that Kathleen was just sleeping. The nurse was greatly concerned that I might be upset or hysterical. I wasn't. I was sad. I didn't feel as if my mother had passed away. It just felt as if Aunt Kathleen had fallen asleep. The nurse may not even have known that Kathleen was my mother even though I had visited often and been seen regularly. It was lonely, I had missed her passing perhaps only by seconds and I was sad and cross with myself. I asked the nurse if Kathleen had been awake beforehand, thinking if she had been awake might I have spoken to her, if I had been only a little earlier, but the nurse said no, she had been asleep for a while and had just drifted off in her sleep as it were, the nurse probably thought she was still asleep as I came in. This was not a ward like in other hospitals, no screens, no drips, no hookups to monitors, no beep beep beep, no long drawn out flatline beeeeeeeeep.

She just looked so peaceful, tranquil, at ease and natural that I wanted to picture the scene. In a world before mobile phones, I explained that I was going out to the car to get my camera and I would be back in less than a minute. I asked the nurse not to touch Kathleen or to move her in any way, that I wanted to picture her just as she was looking now, like she was just sleeping. Kathleen was still warm so I had not been long talking to the nurse. I rushed out to the car and back.

When I came back into the ward my heart sank. The nurse I spoke to was nowhere to be seen. There was a senior or sister or matron pulling the curtains around the bed. They had moved Kathleen, changed her hair, folded her arms across her chest, with a rosary beads around her hands. Two candles at bedsides completed the Catholic poise that was required. She looked like a dead woman. She was cold. I tried to explain to the sister what I had said to the nurse and what I had wanted. 'Oh we can't be doing that,' said the sister firmly. I looked but couldn't find the nurse, probably just as well as I might have gotten her into trouble.

I was very annoyed by what had been done, but probably I shouldn't have been. I should however have been more annoyed with myself for not getting there even five minutes earlier. She might have woken to me, might have said a few words, she might not. I will never know.

I took my few photographs and left. It wasn't Aunt Kathleen anymore, she was gone. There was a dead person in the bed.

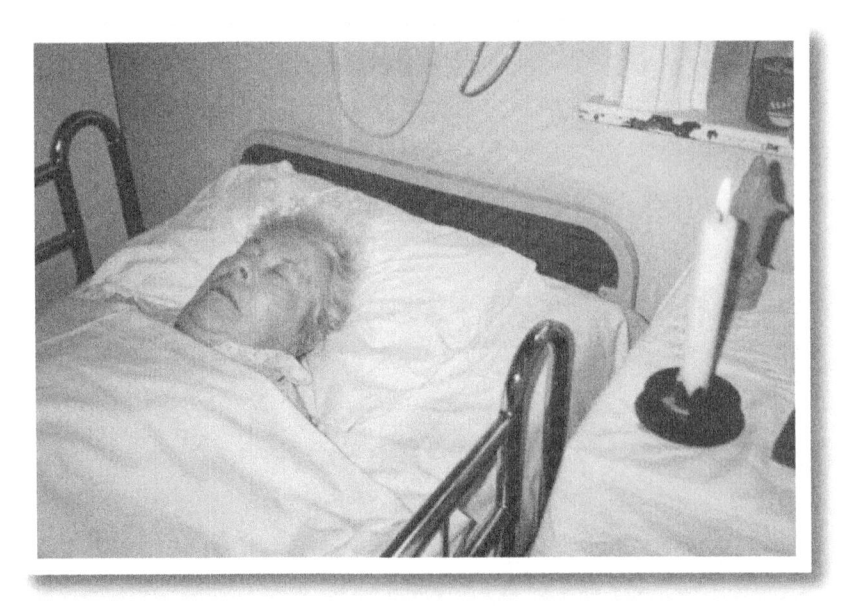

Kathleen just after she had passed away, in Donnybrook Hospital 1994.

A Bit of a Message
Sat 13th August 1994

Kathleen died in Donnybrook hospital on Thursday 11th of August 1994. Her funeral took place two days later at the church of the Assumption Dalkey, the church which she herself had attended much of her life while she lived in St Begnet's Villas nearby. She had lived there minding the children following the unexpected passing of Veronica who was married to Kathleen's brother Dessie.

The funeral was arranged and organised not by me but by Des and family. In fact Des had also been instrumental years earlier and getting Kathleen admitted to Donnybrook Hospital after she had had a few turns and her health had started to fail. Dessie Swords for most of his life had famously been the clerk of the church in Dalkey so presumably his being well-known in church and diocesan circles helped, he had all the right contacts. Anyway Dessie and his family organised the funeral, and even though Kathleen was my mother, it didn't feel like I was at my mother's funeral at all. It felt like it was Aunt Kathleen's funeral. I felt a bit on the edge of it all.

Among my family, friends and acquaintances, I assumed most people knew Kathleen was my mother. Among a wider public in Dalkey who knew Kathleen, I did not know who knew, neither they nor me spoke about it much or acknowledged it publicly. They all had busy lives to live and the truth of it did not preoccupy them. Maybe I was the only one thinking about it everyday.

Years later I was to discover that in Dalkey virtually everyone who knew Kathleen would have known of Kathleen's child, it was not that uncommon in those times. Dalkey is a small close gossipy community, where everyone, especially in one's own social strata, knew everyone else, and everything about them, even if they weren't talking openly about it. No secrets in Dalkey, nowhere to hide. A typical closed Irish community.

The funeral was organised at fairly short notice. We travelled to Donnybrook Hospital for the removal then out to Dalkey church for the funeral. The interment took place after Mass at Deansgrange Cemetery, burial with her parents Patrick and Ellen Swords. There was a good crowd at the funeral, the whole extended Swords family and many neighbours, friends and acquaintances, even though Kathleen had been out of circulation in Dalkey for a long time while she was in Donnybrook Hospital, but Kathleen was well known in Dalkey and well thought of by all who knew her. The singer for the funeral mass was booked and was singing in the organ loft. The hymns were magnificent. The readings were arranged, I did one reading and I think Rosemary Swords did another. I had asked the priest earlier if I could select my reading from

Kathleen, at the time she moved to Dalkey to help rear the young children and keep the family together, after Aunt Veronica passed away too young. Seen here with Paula and Rosemary Swords.

anywhere appropriate, including the Gospels, as usually the Gospels are only read by the priest. He said fine, work away. So I chose a piece to mark the occasion and to make a subtle statement, a declaration, whether widely understood or not.

So I chose from John, 25th, 26th, 27th.

Near the cross of Jesus there stood his Mother, his Mother's sister, Mary the wife of Clopas, and Mary Magdalene.

Seeing His mother there with the Disciple whom he loved, Jesus said to his Mother, Woman there is your Son.

In turn he said to the Disciple, there is your Mother. From that hour onwards the Disciple took her into his care.

It was a subtle statement, a bit of a message. I read it slowly, clearly and deliberately. I didn't know if anyone got it, maybe it was too subtle, but I was glad I had chosen it and read it from the altar.

After I had read it, while someone else was reading I stood beside the lectern looking down into the congregation. There were two old dears sitting about four rows back, with no one sitting in front of them, the type of dear old ladies who probably attended daily Mass and probably always sat in the same seat. One leaned over and whispered to the other, while nodding her head towards me. I couldn't hear what was being said, but I could work out what it might be.

'That's him, that's her son you know. That's Kathleen's Child'. I could not be sure but it made sense to me.

After the funeral mass we all mingled and talked inside the church and outside, there were no people rushing to shake my hand or sympathize as might occur for a chief mourner with any other Mother's funeral. It wasn't my Mother's funeral, it was Aunt Kathleen's funeral. In a way it was a happy funeral, not sad, for everyone there knew and loved Aunt Kathleen. For me it felt strange and I did not feel like 'The Son', as might be the case at another Mother's funeral, Kathleen had been my mother all my life yet had only been the Mother I knew about for the last 7 years, for many of which she had been in Donnybrook Hospital. It all felt very strange to me, I didn't know quite how to feel. I was not upset or tear filled as one might be at other close funerals. I spoke to people outside the church not knowing who knew or didn't know, or cared. It was like being in attendance at the funeral of someone you knew but were not close to, like you had dropped into just any other funeral. I was with Jacinta who was great in helping me, but she was constantly being spoken to and distracted by friends and acquaintances, old neighbours and old friends of Kathleens, so I was sometimes wandering in the crowd of mourners, a bit lost. Eventually I found John, put my head on his shoulder and

A Bit of Unusual Activity.
On the Nightlines Booterstown
1957 or 1958

I grew up in Booterstown until I was nearly ten. In Pembroke Cottages, a small L shaped group of Artisan Dwellings, small houses just off Booterstown Avenue. Among the Cottages, a group of men, the daddies in the houses, were keen fishermen, not the fine art of aristocratic fly-fishing but the coarser more working class art of sea fishing, beach casting. They often travelled to the famous fishing beaches of Wexford, where they would fish on the beaches, often all night long with tents, lights, and massive fishing rods, Beachcasters, that would cast out huge distances to the deeper waters where the big fish swam, hopefully. Our next door neighbours Molly and Ned Kenny, and their son, Young Ned, led the expertise in this fishing activity, and Molly in the kitchen after the fishing.

Closer to home they often fished on Booterstown Strand at the bottom of Booterstown Avenue, crossing the railway line and on out to the huge shallow sandy beach, not fishing with rods, they were nightlining. This form of fishing, suited to big shallow beaches, involved getting on to the beach as the tide was going out. The beach was very flat and the outgoing tide went out a long way before turning to come in again. Catching the tide just right often meant leaving home at two or three in the morning and walking out over the rippled sand a long way to where the tide was virtually fully out. This was the point where the nightline was laid, at the turning point of the tide. The long line was laid flat on the sand. It had many short lines attached to it, with hooks secured on each short line, maybe as many as forty or fifty. These were quickly baited with Rag worm or Lugworm which had been dug on this same beach in the days before. The long line, sometimes called a Spinnet in other parts of Ireland, was staked firmly in the sand with long metal stakes so as not to be swept away by the incoming tide. The idea of laying the line at this point was to wait until the tide turned and started to come in and cover the line and the baited hooks, otherwise the seagulls would take all the bait. The group, maybe four or five men including Old Ned Kenny, Young Ned Kenny, Pat Swords, Paddy Cardiff, Andy Murphy and a couple of chiselers including me and other youngsters, would walk in ahead of the incoming tide. This could be dangerous as the tide on such a beach did not always come in straight and steady, sometimes it was slow, sometimes it rushed ahead or around the walkers cutting them off, a dangerous event if it happened. To say nothing of the dreaded Cockle Lake, a notorious area of liquid soft sand rumoured to have taken a few lost souls down to a dreadful end. Just as well we had a couple of experienced fishermen, 'old salts', to guide us in.

The tide came in to full, the lines were covered and in the deep water over the line the big fish took the bait and were hooked.

We of course were home in bed at this stage, but not for long. We had to be up, awake, and back down on the beach to walk out the outgoing tide to the line. Sometimes we had attached a float on a long line tied to a first or last stake to guide us to where the line was laid. It was critical to reach the line before it was fully uncovered, otherwise the gulls would have taken whatever fish were caught. And a lot of fish were often caught, this was a good, effective and well tried method of fishing, it felt medieval or even prehistoric in its simplicity, who knows.

A great variety of fish were caught, Plaice, Dabs, Turbot, Lemon Sole, Salmon Bass, Dogfish and occasionally a small Shark. If the mackerel were in, you caught a million, otherwise none. All had to be taken off the hooks and into large plastic buckets and bags. We discarded some at this stage, such as dogfish, not for eating. Those we wanted were gutted and cleaned in the salt water, as the gulls swirled all around us, waiting for us to leave the table, their turn to eat. Sometimes at this point the hooks were rebaited and the cycle repeated. On a 'Big Fish' event there might be two or even three nightlines to be serviced. However, many times the lines had been broken and damaged beyond reuse, and far out on the beach at the turning tide was not a good time or place to be undertaking repairs.

We walked, struggled, back over the long beach laden down with fish. Back up Booterstown Avenue, often with more fish than we knew what to do with. Depending on the time of the tides, this could be at six or seven in the morning. The fish was not caught for selling, it was for consumption and for sharing with friends and neighbours in the Cottages. Often it was all brought up to our house, Number Seven, and the work began there. A few of the other wives such as Molly Kenny came in and joined May Swords, the process of cutting, washing and cooking began. This work had to be done quickly. There wasn't a fridge to save your life in the Cottages, maybe in the Quality Houses up and down the Avenue there might have been a Kelvinator or a Frigidaire, we knew about them from American magazines, but we didn't know or mix or talk to the people in the Quality Houses. No, we were the people who kept our butter and milk in stone troughs of cold water, stood on a cold granite floor, a practice, like the fishing, probably unchanged since Medieval times. So a great deal of the fish had to be cooked and eaten quickly whatever the time. It could be eight or nine in the morning, all hands on deck, maybe three or four frying pans on the go, three or four cooks all engaged furiously. The sounds and smells of frying fish was overwhelming, for breakfast! What wasn't being cooked and eaten was wrapped up as 'giveaways', a bundle of fish wrapped in sheets of The Evening Press and distributed to neighbours in the Cottages. They would have to do their own cooking. All the bundles would be gratefully received - recycling 1950's style. Meanwhile the men and boys, and women off duty on the frying pans, tucked into a huge breakfast of Salmon Bass cutlets, floured and fried. I remember those furious unusual breakfasts, the sounds, the smells, the laughing chatter for all of my life. Fortunately I loved fish, still do, if you didn't like fish you were in the wrong house. Huge amounts of fish, strong tea and white and brown bread, with lashings of butter were devoured with tales of the even bigger fish we caught, or didn't caught, once. In a lull, maybe a story about a tragic loss at the Cockle Lake just to frighten the youngsters, or to teach them something.

Later in the morning the youngster's job was to distribute the 'giveaway' fish parcels to friends and neighbours, often resulting in a handsome tip for the messenger. Later the men might repair to the pub for pints and 'small ones' to discuss the night and any plans for more fishing.

The wives would clean up the table, the kitchen, and the house, many hands making light work. Then, glad to be shut of the men, they would sit down together at the table to more tea, and get stuck in to some serious gossip. It took most of the day to recover from a successful 'Nightlining' night.

A Bit Brave or What ?
1956

I suppose I was five or 6 when it happened. I remembered this all the years without fully understanding it. I never tried to figure out what it was all about until something similar occurred years later when I was about 14. Then I recalled the earlier event again and gave it some more thought.

Around age 5 or 6 I was at a kind of concert in the local school I attended . I was there in High Babies and First Class and the event was a school concert, a fundraiser. It was organised by the teachers, nuns and staff and featured a lot of the school kids and parents, a Variety Show I guess you'd call it. Class groups singing, dancing, playing recorders and flageolets. Some of the parents put on Little plays or funny sketches. It was all dreadfully amateurish and awful but I was too young to know these words or what they meant. It was an unusual and exciting event and I was loving it. The idea of leaving the house in the dark evening and walking to the school nearby which had all the lights on was great, it felt very different to the junior school as I knew it from school in the daytime. It was strange to see classmates out of the classroom. Some of the Mammys I recognised. Strange too to see teachers and nuns out of class laughing and smiling. They weren't supposed to be happy, they were supposed to be strict. I don't remember who brought me.

I was with Ma and some of the neighbouring wives. Da was somewhere else, in fact there weren't many Da's there at all. The hall was all lit up and there was a great hubbub of people talking and calling to each other. Next thing the lights went down and it all went very quiet. Only the stage was lit up. The whole place was dark and I felt just a little apprehensive. I was sitting on a seat by the centre aisle, with a good view of the stage. The different acts came on and sang, danced or played something. I clapped when everyone else clapped, laughed when everyone else laughed. A man came on and juggled balls and other things and he got a clap. Then when he dropped things or when the balls rolled off the stage he got a bigger clap, a cheer, and a big laugh. I clapped, cheered, and laughed but I didn't understand why. There was a break then when the lights came up, for a raffle, whatever that was. Then the lights went down and it got really really dark, even the stage went dark except for a little small light. A couple appeared on the stage in the very dark and walked across the stage in a very staggering way like drunks, with arms linked. They talked to each other in a slurred voice and sat on a garden bench on the stage. They started singing a song together – 'when the Red Red Robin goes Bob Bob Bobbin along…..' They were awful singers but they got a laugh and a clap. I didn't clap, I was nervous.
Then out of the shadows at the back of the stage a ghosty thing appeared. A huge white sheet with big black eyes and stalky arms and hands came out slowly behind the couple while they were singing. They kept on singing about the Red Red Robin.

The people in the seats laughed and shouted out 'behind you, behind you'. The singers looked puzzled and asked What? Where? The ghosty thing slipped into the background. The singers sang again.. 'goes Bob Bob Bobbing along'. The ghosty thing came out again, closer now it put its bony hand on the man's shoulder. He didn't notice. There were louder shouts of 'behind you'. The couple were still puzzled. The man got up and said to the people in the seats What? Where? Next time the ghosty thing appeared behind the seat it put two arms around the couple. They felt the arms, the hands, they looked around and saw the ghosty thing and jumped up startled. They ran around the stage in a panic, the ghosty thing chased them around the stage. They bumped into each other and the ghosty thing and they all fell down. Up again, more chasing, all the people in the hall were shouting and laughing. I wasn't. I was terrified. The couple ran off the stage one each side and down into the hall. The ghosty thing followed them, chasing down into the hall. When they all ran down the hall near to my seat, my seat was empty. I was gone. I had jumped up out of my seat terrified, down the hall, out the door and ran home to where I lived. There was no one home, so all I could do was sit waiting on the doorstep crying in the dark. Eventually I was missed and someone came looking for me and waited with me until other people came home. I didn't want to talk about it and no one wanted to make me talk about it. Someone said 'don't be silly', that's all.

Many years later I was in the local cinema, The Astoria in Glasthule with some of the lads watching some vampire film. There was lots of teeth, blood and blood red eyes and screams. I felt that terror again. I got up, got out of my seat, said nothing to my friends, turned and walked out into the cold night air, and kept going. I remembered the ghosty thing from the school hall of many years ago and also leaving that hall. It might have been said that I should have been brave and stayed to watch on both occasions. But I reckon it took a lot of brave to get up and go, not to watch something that upset me. I reckon I was brave enough to go and not to worry about what others thought, either the lads or the mammys. When I thought about it more, I saw that I didn't care what anyone thought. That was brave.

A Bit of a Great Time When We Were the Boys
The Boy's Club
1964

A really important and formative part of my childhood was the time I spent with the boy's club in Glasthule. Only many years later, looking back through adult eyes, can I see its true worth. This piece gives a small look back at what it was like.

'Are you goin' Tuesday night'
'Sure am. Wouldn't miss it'
'Ok, I'll see you there'.

The 'it' and the 'there' was The Club. Saint Brendan's Boys Club to be exact, held at night twice a week, in a prefab building on what was once the tennis courts of a former Grand House called Beaufort, in Glasthule, or Sandycove as it was probably known when the Big House was in its heyday. Sandycove was thought to be a superior upper class name for the area, whereas Glasthule was seen as downmarket and working class. Saint Brendan's Boys Club was definitely in Glasthule and all that that implied, at the time we joined it. In the early sixties with us around twelve to fourteen we wanted more than anything to join The Club. Most of our friends, the lads we played with on the streets every day, and their older brothers were in or about to join the club. To join was a rite of passage at this age, it was necessary for a young fella to be in the club, to be accepted, to be part of the club community, to be one of the lads. So, down the road we went and spoke to one of the Brothers to ask to join. We were spoken for by some of the existing members, or maybe vouched by some of the Leaders, older boys, who knew us. The older lads, maybe sixteen or seventeen at that time to our thirteen or fourteen, seemed like men to us. The few years age gap at this age was huge, the big lads were grown up and we looked up to them.

So we joined and started going to the club nights. It was great to belong, and to be going out at night, with the lads, in a safe and well run organisation, to be growing up. The Mammies were glad we were in the club and safe, and not running the roads and getting into trouble. Being adults the Mammies knew the club was good for us, teaching us community, respect for others and character building in growing up. We weren't mature enough to see this, we just wanted to have fun and to belong like all the other lads.

The club was run by the local branch of The Society of Saint Vincent de Paul, so it was intended to provide an outlet and a form of education to the poor children of working class families. But then we didn't see ourselves as poor or if we were we didn't know it. No, we were just like everyone else. We knew we weren't rich, we knew we had no money, but we were rich in our family lives of simple food, good stories and books, and parents that were outgoing and curious, who took us on long walks and told us local history and ghost stories. All this we realized much later as we grew up. At the time our parents knew that the club was good for us, but we just wanted to have fun, and to belong.

My cousin John had joined the club a year before me, he was about a year older. John lived in Sallynoggin a few miles away, but spent so much time visiting and playing with me in Findlater Street Glasthule as to make him almost a real 'Glasthuler', so he was in. I then joined with him and our local friends from the streets.

Most of the lads lived around the immediate area of Glasthule, Congress Gardens, Devitt Villas, O'Donnell Gardens, Eden Terrace, Findlater Street (where I lived), Coldwell Street, and the notorious and sometimes rough Eden Villas known as The Hundred and One (101 houses). Some of the bigger lads from the hundred were great characters – Yaadi Deveraux, Tiddler Meagan, Freddy Glynn, and Babby Martin - were like gods to us youngsters, not tough guys but kindly colourful characters. The men who managed and ran the club were firm but fair, men with families of their own giving their time and care freely as Society members, they were not 'Religious' but were referred to as 'Brothers'. Being in the VdeP, running the club was for them a form of vocation. They were good men and true, and we recall them fondly, Dick Hanrahan, Anthony Kennedy,

Martin Lynch, Johnny Reilly, Robert Thomas and the old man himself, Doc Fleming.

There were 'Fathers' too in that some of the local parish curates attended in a pastoral function, like Father McCabe, Niall Makey, and Fr.Paul McLaughlin. I don't recall any preaching or much praying activity other than the saying of the Rosary to close some nights (during which it was impossible to suppress the 'giggles' when someone near made a funny remark, almost a 'mortaler' if you were caught). Some of the bigger lads, seventeen or eighteen, acted as 'Leaders', helping with supervision and control if needed, which it sometimes was.

Activities in the club varied over the year, summer bright evenings we often played soccer, or rounders on what were once the tennis courts of the old grand house. Rounders, a good game to include a lot of boys, was like a form of baseball, great fun until someone hit a mighty swing sending the ball way out of the grounds and lost in a neighbour's back garden. But we never played cricket, didn't speak with the right accent or go to the right schools. On darker wintry evenings we were obliged to work indoors, often at woodwork classes. These classes were given by a kindly retired gentleman, Mr Doherty, whose heart I'm sure we broke with our smart alecky remarks and lack of application to follow his instructions, especially anything that required attention to detail or patience, like sanding a piece of wood for an hour, or making carpentry joints. The finer points of dovetail joints were wasted on us – 'but a dove doesn't have a wooden tail like that' – we cracked a smart answer in our ignorance. The poor man, I hope he got his reward in Heaven. We were also introduced to basket weaving, foreign to us, but we soon got the hang of it and made some lovely pieces. I made a nice four legged stool with a woven latticed seat. I brought it home proud as punch. It was very useful for Da to put his feet up on to lace a boot or to polish his good shoes. It lasted a good while until it started to break, then it went on the fire.

In a part of the big room, between it and the games room was a corner with a radio and a record player. This area where the records and radio were played was the music area run strictly and controlled by Joe. Joe Jackson that was, and fair do's to him for being in charge of this because he owned the record player, and all the records. In fairness to Joe while he did sometimes, mostly, dominate this activity, he was entitled to as he put so much into it. Besides which Joe really knew his music, it was his passion. While we couldn't know it at the time, probably Joe didn't know it either, he would go on in later life to have a distinguished career as a music journalist of note and interviewer of many famous names of stage, film, and the world of music. An author, playwright, and a performer of one man stage shows based on his lifetime of interviews, received to great acclaim. But all that was in the future for Joe, in his corner in the club he picked and played the records, his records. Now Joe was HUGE into Elvis (still is), but not all of us were the same.

Many a night we suffered on through 'Wooden Heart' and 'Blue Suede Shoe', and said nothing, afraid to complain. They say – whoever 'they' are – that the music you love around age 12 to 14 is the music you will love all your life. In this I am indebted to Joe for introducing me to the first LP of the Rolling Stones, the one with the black and white photo cover and memorable songs like Carol, Little Red Rooster and Route 66, still great. We also got to know The Animals – House of the Rising Sun – The Yardbirds - For Your Love - The Kinks – Lola, Dedicated Follower of Fasion, Waterloo Sunset -and others, favourites for a lifetime, introduced to us by Joe. Even Elvis, he wasn't too bad, after a while. Thanks Joe.

Through the door from the 'Music Corner', took you into the billiard room, the Holy of Holies for those of us who liked to play billiards. It was small, cramped and contained an old quarter sized Billiard table which had seen better days. You only went in there to play or to watch billiards. To others, non players, it was boring. But to the players it was great. Mostly, but not always, it was a place of hushed respect, no drinks to spill, no eating crisps over the table. And a strict protocol was followed as to who got to play. If there was a game of two players on the table and you wanted to play soon, you declared 'up next', at which stage you probably did the marking, or keeping score for the current game, and you played the winner. So a player, who kept winning, kept playing. You soon got to know who were the 'sharks' and against whom you had little chance. Still, it was good to play, if only to get beaten, you got to learn how to play, and how to lose. The table was not as they say the 'Mae West', often there was a slope or a 'run' to one side or the other requiring bits of cardboard or wedges from the woodworking class to straighten things up. Also, there were sight cracks in the slate or 'bed' of the table. These might reappear if the table got a knock making an almost invisible ridge in the green baize cloth. If you were good, or cute, you could subtly take advantage of these features before they were corrected. Sometimes the ball travelled to the pocket in a very nearly straight line. Playing Billiards in the Boys Club taught us a lot about life – play the game fairly but take advantage of any breaks that came your way – you learn quickly. I still play Billiards nearly sixty years later.

The Boys Club did us good and taught us many lessons while we thought we were just having fun. But there was more, there was 'The Holiday'.

The holiday was the highlight of the club year. Most of us boys in the club were not from families who were of the type who went on holidays, anywhere, more hand to mouth, week to week. I had never been on a holiday in the usual sense. I had been taken on a long weekend with relatives, to Villierstown, Cappoquin, County Waterford, to a primitive village with one street. It was indeed primitive, no electricity in the homes, no piped water – a bucket from the well, no indoor flushing toilets

– an outhouse with a plank over a hole in the ground, and cut up newspapers hanging on a nail, a huge fireplace you could walk right into with an all day blazing turf fire. Cooking pots, bastibles and griddles hung on fire crane irons swinging over the red hot turf. It was primitive, like going back in time four hundred years to another Ireland. I didn't know enough at the time to treasure the memory and romantic nostalgia of it all. I just knew that the toilet stank and I didn't want to go there. But the Club Holiday was not going to be anything like that the lads said, so I was all for it.

Usually a week's holiday in August was organised by the Brothers well in advance and the price established so we could save, beg, borrow or steal the money, but we had to go. In earlier years the holiday took the boys to large houses in the countryside, places like Lonan Murphy House in Kildare that might formerly have been schools or convents, now available to the SVdeP to bring boys like us to for holidays, with dormitory accommodation for thirty or forty boys. A week in the countryside for young boys from Glasthule, playing at the riverside, bringing in the hay, it was beyond their wildest dreams, another world.

The club holidays I went on took us to a rambling unfinished and falling down accommodation on top of a cliff of sand dunes overlooking the huge beach of Gormanston, north of Dublin, in County Meath. Once the holiday was named and dated and the price set, we set about putting our names down and getting the money. The dates never clashed with our parents plans, our parents had no plans. Some of us, John and I for example, worked as lounge boys in the Eagle House pub in Glasthule and so we could save a few bob towards the price of the holiday, which wasn't too expensive as it was subsidised by the VdeP Society. The money was begged, borrowed (family), and stolen (Eagle House) and we were nearly there. We always had more than we let on, and at the end we were discreetly given extra money by aunts and uncles (don't tell your mother). All set, we were going. The price was all in for accommodation, breakfast and dinner, and trips. We would always be out for lunch, at our own expense, so you made sure to eat everything you could find for breakfast, including someone else's breakfast, if you could get away with it.

The day came. Meeting at Sandycove and Glasthule railway station, on the train into Amiens Street station, change trains, then northwards and stop at the small halt of Gormanston station. A short walk up a hill took us to the place we were to stay in, Stillman's. We didn't know enough to deal with what met us. It was awful. It was great. It was newly built. It was nearly built. Bare floors of cement. Bare walls of concrete block. Nearly all the windows were in. But we didn't care – we were on The Holiday. 'Look, it's on top of a sand dune hill leading down to the biggest beach ever. The sun is shining – 'last one in is a cissy!'

We changed quickly, ran down the sand dunes and out over the beach to the water's edge. Many of us stopped, realizing it was colder than we expected. But many of us plunged on in, cold and all as it was. 'It's great once you're numb with the cold' we shouted to the others to join us. Eventually when we were not only numb but blue as well we made our way back to the dormitories, sticky with sand, we changed into anything warm, no showers, no hot water, with fresh clothes, sort of, we were ready and looking forward to dinner later, with big appetites we were ready to eat for Ireland. Tons of chips and burgers – were no problem. At the end of our first day of The Holiday we were stuffed and exhausted. We had a quiz and many of us played cards or draughts. Off to bed, tired, the beds were wrought iron framed bunks in separate dorms of six bunks each, bare block walls, in the cold we wrapped ourselves in hairy blankets, coats and anoraks to get warm. 'Keep your socks on' someone suggested, we didn't need to be told twice, it worked.

In the dark before we went asleep there was a great deal of shouting bunk to bunk and dorm to dorm. Lewd jokes were shouted out and a sort of farting contest developed. There were some mighty farters in the boys club.

During the week we filled every minute – we played rounders on the beach, we dug caves into the sandy cliffs without knowing the danger we were in, and all the while up and down the

*The Boys Club rescue on Gormanston Beach.
That could be me in the water near the back wheel, trying
to help, but really just getting in the way.*

beach we collected driftwood and scrap for a bonfire to mark the end of the holiday. Sometimes something unexpected happened. Coming back from a long beach walk scavenging we found someone had driven their car too far out on the beach and with the tide coming in fast the car was stuck and the water was rising up the wheels. A rescue was underway when we arrived. A local man had been contacted and he was driving his tractor up the beach to the rescue. This was great, we had to join in the rescue effort. Those of us who could, changed into swimming togs and foolishly tried to help, we were more in the way. The tractor eased into the rising tide and attempts were made to attach a rope line to the car. What we didn't realize was that with the car and now the tractor well into the water everything stank of diesel fuel, including us. Those of us who had accidently taken a gulp of water or dived under were now busy getting sick into the water we stood in. And we stayed sick long into the night, long after the car had been pulled from the water and been pulled home by the tractor. The car was ruined but out, and the tractor driver was heading for the pub compliments no doubt of the car owner. The tractor driver would soon be telling the lads in the bar about the eejit who drove the car out too far, and about all the other eejits of young fellas getting sick in the water. We didn't care what he might have been saying, we were still sick.

Two excursions were organised for us during the week of the holiday. The first was a visit to the local Army Camp and

Gormanston Aerodrome. This was exciting stuff, we could inspect the planes on the ground, small single and double winged aircraft used for reconnaissance in the war, possibly the first war, quite old fashioned looking. We didn't care. We sat in the cockpit, we pulled back on the stick, and we made our own sound effects and rat-tat-tats as we shot down Red Barons or anyone else who got in our sights. We even wore an old fashioned leather flying helmet we found under a seat – we were cool.

Also on the camp we got to visit and play around the rifle ranges, not in use at the time. Still, we could imagine ourselves shooting. Up around the massive targets we found loads of spent bullets, well the top parts, the parts that killed you. They were on the ground, in the clay bank behind the targets, and many in the targets themselves, someone was a good shot. Now we could imagine ourselves shooting, and we had pockets full of bullets to make it seem real. We took home loads and many of us kept them for years. The whole visit was beyond cool, it was like being in a story in the Hotspur or Commando, the comics we read at home.

The second excursion and the highlight of The Holiday was a visit to Butlin's Holiday Camp, in Mosney, just up the road from Gormanston. We had heard of Butlins, the well known indoor and outdoor holiday camp much beloved of British working class 'campers' in the North of England, now newly arrived here with their first holiday camp in Ireland in Mosney. We had

*Group of boys and Brothers on a Boy's Club Holiday,
visiting Gormanston Airfield to look at the planes, and hopefully
not fly them.*

never been to visit or stay in such a place, it would have been beyond the pockets of our parents. But here we were on a day trip, everything, rides and admissions paid for, all we needed was a few bob spending money. It was a wondrous place with so many things to do that you didn't know where to start. Outdoor amusement parks, crazy golf, Helter Skelter, paddle boats on the lake, roller skating on a real good rink, not like the broken pavements we skated on back home, train rides all around the park, and all free. A huge outdoor pool with slides into the water. Huge indoor games areas with more snooker, billiards and pool tables than we ever imagined. We gave them a go. Best of all was a huge indoor heated swimming pool. We couldn't wait. Indoors, sort of under the indoor pool was a huge lounge seating area, and most wondrous of all to our eyes while you sat in this area having tea or coca cola one of the walls was a huge glass window, the glass side of the swimming pool above. So you could sit in comfort looking into the pool underwater as the swimmers swam and dived. If the swimmers dived down along the glass they could not see through into the lounge, but we could see the swimmers clearly and spent ages watching them, mostly the girls. We had to try this, in our swimming togs we got into the warm pool and loved it. Some of the lads and other visitors were down in the lounge, a few lads who were swimming swam down to the window and even though they could not see through, they managed to line up at the glass, pull down their togs and moon their bare bums to anyone unfortunate to be watching. Afterwards, a few lads who were down in the lounge and saw it said it worked really well, ladies and girls shrieked, complaints were made. The lads said you couldn't tell who was who, they all looked like arses.

There was one other marvellous wonder in Butlins which made a huge impression on me and some of the other lads from the club. It was in a corner of the big lounge under the pool. It was an automatic Ring Doughnut Making Machine, and we were transfixed watching it work. It was a vending machine, you put in your coins, a bob for two or a tanner for one, and watched the wonders taking place. Once the money was in it started up. A ring of raw doughnut mix was extruded and dropped into a tank of hot bubbling oil where it sizzled away for a while turning a golden brown. It was then moved somehow with some kind of paddles out of the cooking oil onto a platform where it drained of oil, sort of, and cooled down a little. Then it was dropped into a tray of sugar and sprinkled with more sugar on top. Finally it was moved around somehow to under a plastic flap, and when a green light went on you could open the plastic flap and take out the still hot doughnut using a napkin which you pulled from the machine. At this point you ate the hot sugary doughnut greedily while you searched your pockets for coins to buy the next one. It was a wonder to behold, like science fiction, like something from a Dan Dare comic – a food making machine – and what food! We loved them and bought more, Babby Martin, who could eat all around him ate six. I had four and felt sick afterwards. On the way home after

Butlins we could not stop talking about the doughnut machine. Many of the lads who missed seeing this wonderful machine were jealous and kept saying 'tell us again', they hardly believed us, but we had the sweet sugary lips and mouths to prove it. I've never seen another one of these machines since.

The next day of our holiday was to be our last; we were going home the following morning. It was a busy day down on the beach with the last push to collect as much stuff for the bonfire as possible, looking for material that might have been washed up on the shore with the last high tides. There were last group photographs to be taken, we were all growing up and some older lads acting as leaders were moving on in life, work or careers, and felt this might be their last club holiday, so the photos were important to remember. Some of us younger lads were saying a long last goodbye to the young girls who worked in the hostel, moonstruck goodbyes could last all day. Asked to join in the bonfire hunt someone else said 'don't ask him, he's in love'. Love for a fourteen year old is a terrible thing.
The night came, it got dark and the bonfire was lit and burned on for hours, it was huge. The Brothers and leaders kept an eye on things and made sure the younger lads did not do anything stupid. What the young lads did not see or realize was the wonderful freedom they had building and burning the bonfire, this was not a secret sneaky thing to be hidden like a Halloween fire back home, with the neighbours, police and fire brigade out to stop it. No this was a creative expression, a celebration of the

great holiday, which was to be enjoyed and remembered. This was a lesson they had not realized yet, that they were learning by being part of Saint Brendan's Boys Club on holiday. No one was drunk or drinking or needed to be to make it better. The bonfire blazed brightly till late in the night, eventually collapsing in on itself, until it was only glowing embers, hardly making enough light to help us see our way up the sand dune bank to head for bed. It was a great ending.

It was the last night of the holiday before going home and it was hard to get to sleep. Spirits were high and there was even more shouting of lewd jokes and singing of bawdy songs. There was a great deal of wandering around in pj's, or jocks, or nothing's, to annoy lads in other dorm room by pulling off bedclothes or splashing water on half sleeping bodies and hopefully escaping fast so that the 'splashers' could not be identified by the 'splashees', for revenge later. Eventually even the diehard pranksters got tired and fell asleep, not always in their own beds but anywhere. Some woke at fourish a.m. wondering why they were stretched out on the floor or even under a bottom bunk. Rising early the following morning many washed in cold water, most didn't. Breakfast was as much cornflakes as you could get your hands on, and many many cups of tea, all bolted down. Packing to go home was a battleground, with accusations of stolen socks, shoes and assorted clothing almost starting a row. Many items of clothing were lost for good, most likely lost in the sand dunes. We marched, singing, to the small railway halt of Gormanston and

the train back to Glasthule. A strange mixture of happy and sad prevailed, and we agreed that the holiday was great, probably the best ever, said some of the older lads who had been on previous holidays. But we all agreed that next year's holiday would be even better, we'd explore further up the beach, and the bonfire would be even bigger next year. We might even get to Butlins twice, could you imagine that. We arrived back at Sandycove and Glasthule Railway Station and as we trudged up the sloping path to the way out, one last photograph of the group was taken.
We were home.

As we grew older we eventually grew out of the club. Some of the older lads stayed on as leaders keen to give something back to the place they got so much from. Others of us as we grew up fell by the wayside, distracted by girls, or having a grown up drink in some dark and dingy pub. But even though we left, the club never really left us. Some of the Brothers helped us find holiday jobs or even real fulltime work, still looking out for us. We met some of them elsewhere after we left, we stopped and chatted with them and they were always interested in how we were getting on after the club. It took us a good while of growing up before we appreciated how much we had gotten from the club, some skills, some confidence, some camaraderie, friends for life. We didn't meet regularly for a long time as our paths diverged, and it was a good time later when many of us met again at the annual 'reunion' drinks at Christmas in the

Eagle House. The Brothers who looked after us and looked out for us have passed away.

Of the leaders, boys maybe only five years older than us, many have passed on also. Even some of the boys we were with while in the Club, boys our own age, have passed on. We raise a glass to them all. And we remember fondly Saint Brendan's Boys Club to which we seemed to give so little and yet we got so much from without realizing it - forever thankful.

We were the boys, Saint Brendan's Boys.

At the end of The Holiday.
Boys from St. Brendan's Boys Club arriving home from Gormanston to Glasthule and Sandycove railway station.

A Bit of Outer Space from Sputnik to Mars
1957

I remember it clearly. 1957, I was 7. Myself and Da watched Sputnik passing over our backyard in Pembroke Cottages in Booterstown.

The backyard was pitch dark at night, no light from the scullery. No street lights shining over the wall, black dark as they say, black as the hob of hell. It was October 4th 1957 so it must have been well dark, and the sky must have been clear and starry. Why Da brought me out to see it I don't know, he wasn't particularly space or tech minded. Perhaps he heard something on the radio news, maybe saying Sputnik could be seen passing over Ireland around 8 o'clock.

We almost never went out into the dark backyard at night. It could be dark and cold, you might trip or slip on an icy or frosty patch. Apart from going down the path to the Lav, or Da nipping out for a log or firewood for the fire, these were usually brought in early before darkness set in, we didn't go out. Going out to the lav was different. A lit candle in a jam jar was carried, nothing fancy or silver. The flickering light was essential to find the door in the dark and to light up the inside so you could find the cut up sheets of the Evening Press hanging on the nail. Without the cut up newspaper you might have to use the packet of Izel, the hardest, scratchiest, awfulest toilet paper ever invented. Tear the bum off you it would. No, the newspaper was much softer. It was very cold out there so you didn't hang around. Rushing back into the house you hoped you wouldn't trip or drop the candle or let it flicker out. There were no torches in most houses, not like today when you can have a bright torch on your keyring. The torches or lights that were in some houses, were for the bicycles, attached to the bike and powered by the Dynamo driven by the front wheel. You couldn't ride your bike to the lav, a candle in a jar would have to do. So, there we were in the dark in the cold backyard, a black starry sky above around the expected time, when we saw it. In 1957 nothing moved in the sky at night. Maybe a shooting star, which were very rare. Not an aeroplane either. We occasionally saw an old plane or a biplane in the daytime, like something lost from WWI or WWII, struggling home. But never a silvery tube modern commercial aeroplane, and never at night. Sputnik was like something we had never seen before. Against the black sky it was just like a star but a bit brighter and bigger than most of the stars, and moving in the sky where nothing else moved. It wasn't moving too fast or too slow or erratically, just moving steadily in a straight line towards the East. It was moving from the Dublin mountains towards the sea at Booterstown Strand and heading on to Holyhead, Wales and England I think. There was no sound, no rockets that we could hear. I learned years later that there was a beep... beep... beep... sound coming from it but they were radio sounds being transmitted from Sputnik and picked up by radio. I heard them years later being played on the radio as it happened, but on the night there was no sound, only silence.

Then it was gone. We watched it getting smaller and smaller as it got further and further away. It was all over quickly. Less than a minute, a good bit less than a minute. That was it. We were told later that history was made that night but we weren't sure how. The following days we saw pictures and drawings of Sputnik in the newspapers. It looked like a big shiny football with long spiky things pointing off it backwards. We had no idea how big it was or how it shone in the sky that night.
But we had seen it and we wouldn't forget it.
We heard more about it but didn't understand all the to-do and goings on about Russia and America and who was winning what. I was going to school and was busy and distracted and Da was wondering if there will be any work next week. Life went on. Sputnik was the first Russian word I knew, soon there would be others. Laika the first dog that went into space – in all the celebrations they never told us that the dog died either in space or on landing – I suppose a Russian dog didn't matter in the grand scheme of things. And Yuri Gagarden as we said it, the first man in space, another Russian. Maybe we could have seen Laika passing over, or Yuri heading for Holyhead, but we didn't. We had seen the one that mattered. The first Sputnik.

We have come a long long way since Sputnik October 1957.

We've been to the moon so many times it has become boring. We've sent rockets to the planets. We've landed spacecraft on Asteroids and on Comets. We've sent so many satellites orbiting around the earth it's like a junkyard up there. All this to operate our mobile phones, internet, and satellite TV giving us millions of channels. All this human ingenuity, skill and outlandish expense to give us TV that is shoddy, shallow, and unworthy. Millions of channels and nothing on. Are any lives being saved or is it all just entertainment. A long way indeed from Sputnik. I am here writing this remembering Sputnik, on the 19th of April 2021, 64 years later living in the science fiction we used to read about. I'm writing this as a Wicklow Writers Group Homework Exercise prompted by the news that we have landed a robot craft on Mars from which we have successfully tested the launch of a helicopter drone which will help us to explore the planet Mars more thoroughly. Probably it will help us to find minerals or diamonds or gold or oil or stuff, so that we can make a start on destroying Mars, now that we are well on our way to destroying our own planet Earth.

Sputnik, did you know this was where it was all heading?

A Meeting that was a Bit Mysterious
1963

During the time I spent in St Mary's Primary School in Oatlands in Mount Merrion, I usually made my way to and from school on my own. I never remembered my parents appearing at the school for any reason, including Sports, or Sales of Work fundraisers. St Mary's primary was linked to Oatlands secondary school and the natural progression after primary certificate was to transition automatically to the secondary school. But this was not always the case and many students left after primary cert and did not progress. This could have been for a variety of reasons, including ability, or other family plans to switch schools, perhaps to move into some apprenticeship or move into some work that needed a move into a technical college. I never remember discussing this type of progression with any of my pupil friends. Either it was assumed one would move into the secondary, or else it was a decision made by parents and not for discussion by the boys themselves. St Mary's was a regular Primary School with little in the way of airs of grandeur, although it had a definite air of respectability about it, with uniforms being required, and a sense of quality about it. It wasn't snobbish; there were other schools in the area that had a greater sense of class and elitism about them. They tended to the rugby playing schools, and felt they had a sense of class and academic high standards to uphold, and attracted boys from business, professional elite, maybe families with a legal or medical background. Boys naturally headed for university like their parents before them, at least their fathers before them. On the other hand, other primary schools in the area were decidedly more ordinary and middle class at best. But the secondary school at Oatlands was known as 'The Private', and had a definite sense of its own importance and class. Also it was a fee paying school which tended to reinforce its sense of worth and exclusivity, indicating a standard it created for itself, one which was applied rigorously.

On one particular day around fifth year going into sixth year, the last year of primary, I was surprised to be met at the end of classes by my Mother and Aunt Kathleen. I was walked down to the secondary school and to the office of the Principal, Brother Tallon I think at the time. This visit must have been pre-arranged and I did not know about it, it took me by surprise. The three of us were admitted by the Principal and there was a token amount of conversation, and questions for me, how was I getting on, what subjects did I like best, while the Principal clicked through his notes, I presume teachers reports on me, attendance records, and suchlike. Then I was asked to leave and wait outside the office while the discussion in this mysterious meeting continued. I waited outside for quite a long time as it happened while they kept talking. I didn't know what was being discussed and made no attempt to listen in at the door. It never crossed my mind to listen in, probably I would have been afraid of being caught listening by some other Brother.

Eventually the discussion finished and the door opened and Ma and Aunt Kathleen came out with a good deal of smiling and shaking of hands with the Principal. Even my hand was shaken by the Principal. There was no explanation for me, no telling me what the meeting was all about. We all just headed for home on the bus. It was such an unusual occurrence I should have thought about it more, but I didn't. Not until many years later. I stayed on at the school, did my Primary Exam, and after summer prepared to go back to school. Having gotten my new uniform, as I was growing a lot, I headed back to school, to Oatlands Secondary School, 'The Private'. Many many years later, and well after 'Tea in the Burlington' and all that I learnt there, the memory of waiting outside the principal's office came back to me and with all that I knew, I began to wonder what had really happened that day with Ma and Aunt Kathleen in the principal's office. Probably around the age of 39 or 40 the memories of that mysterious meeting came back to me.

I thought about it in the new knowledge that Aunt Kathleen was my natural birth mother, and that I had been adopted by Ma and Da, Mary and Pat Swords, first informally and then in 1954, formally and fully adopted. During this childhood period Aunt Kathleen was always there, and always involved in my upbringing. Both Ma and Aunt Kathleen, mostly I would guess Aunt Kathleen had aspirations for my education, and were probably instrumental in sending me to St Mary's Primary School in the first place. Aunt Kathleen probably assisted greatly with the costs of this decision to send me to a 'good' school.

So when I thought about the mysterious meeting I can only assume it had to do with my transition from St Mary's Primary to Oatlands Secondary, 'The Private'.

I expect that any special pleading at the mysterious meeting would have involved them explaining to the Principal the true nature of the relationships, Aunt Kathleen, my Mother, and Mary Swords, my adopted mother, and their joint hope to give Martin the best possible chance with a good education. They would have explained to the Principal that young Martin had had no knowledge of the family relationships, hence I was outside the office while this was being discussed. I'm sure also in this special pleading discussion there would have been agreement to maintain the privacy and confidentiality of the situation. Almost certainly the question of fees for moving into 'The Private' would have been discussed. While there may have been some pleading for reduced fees due to the family structure and circumstances, I've no doubt that Aunt Kathleen would have agreed to pay whatever fees were settled on, to the relief of both Ma and of the Principal. The smiles and handshakes at meeting's end I'm sure indicated a satisfactory conclusion all round.

And so I progressed onwards into Oatlands Private secondary school for the next six years, to my Leaving Certificate in 1969, with no knowledge of my complicated family dynamics. To be fair to Brother Tallon the Principal, and others after him,

I knew nothing of this situation and everything proceeded normally. No special preference was extended to me other than normal treatment, whenever I needed to be slapped, often, I was slapped just like everyone else. Looked at from thirty years later, and in the full knowledge of my family structure, it all made perfect sense to me.

At home in 19 Findlater Street.
May Swords, me doing homework, Kathleen Swords.
On May's lap, Caroline Butler, youngest daughter of Ina.
In our house Caroline was always known as 'Ducky'
No one seems to know why.

A Bit of a Mystery

"We, don't know where we're goin'….."

As a family we were often taken on trips to the seaside, walking, by bus or by train. Full family trips with Parents, Aunts, Uncles, and many Cousins. No motor cars for trips, no TV or i pads. We were brought out to make our own fun. Sometimes we just walked the twenty minute walk down to the seafront nearby, to Bug Rock. Other times, such as in this piece the trips were big and unpredictable adventures.

In the late 1950's getting anywhere nice was often a matter of chance. Cars were scarce, especially on our street, and people with cars who might know you and bring you somewhere nice, were scarcer still. A trip to the seaside or into the country by bus was hard work. By the time you got to the bus, waited for it, took the journey and then walked to a spot for a play and a picnic, usually carrying everything you were going to eat and drink, you were exhausted. Then after the rush to get back to the bus for the journey home and a final walk to the house, you were only fit for a lick of the face cloth and off to bed. Still for us young ones all we remembered was the play, the food and the fun. It was our parents and aunts who were exhausted, but they were happy to see us happy.

Luckily we lived near the railway at Glasthule station, so we often took the train to Killiney strand or Bray seafront and that made a day out much easier. We always seemed to take the train southwards to the nice places. There were other places we could go, northwards, and we'd heard of places in that direction, Howth, Donabate, Bettystown or Gormanston, but we never went there. We were spoiled to have such lovely spots just south of us, sometimes we even went as far south as Greystones!

Occasionally however we took a real adventure trip on the Mystery Train. The Mystery Train was a great idea, it started in Amiens Street Station, you paid your fare for the trip, but you didn't know where you were going until you arrived. Large groups of families would take it, Mams and Dads, kids, aunts and uncles, grannies, cousins, neighbour's kids and even the pet dog was known to have travelled. Picnics were made the night before, whole sliced pans of sandwiches put back into their Johnson Mooney wrappers, apples and pears, whole tomatoes, and hard boiled eggs in their shells were packed into carrier bags for later. By the time later came the bananas in the sandwiches had turned black and the tomato and ham sandwiches were wet, soggy and limp. Something to drink was also packed, no wine or champagne here, flasks of hot water, packets of loose tea, and an old teapot which was not good enough to be cried over if it got broken, which often happened. The Mystery Train took us to all kinds of exotic places, Limerick, Kilkenny, Drogheda, passing through smaller towns which we had only ever met in school geography class, towns like Athy, Maynooth, Portlaoise or even Limerick Junction, what kind of a town is that? The Mystery Train was great fun, and there was a great deal of guessing and speculating as to where we might end up. Some of the seasoned Mystery Trainers tried to work things out based on which platform the train was at, which way we left Dublin and what was the first station we passed through. Once I remember we left Dublin and soon passed through a long long long tunnel in the dark. Someone said we were passing through an old and little used line under the Phoenix Park, maybe we were, but I don't remember now where we ended up.

What I do remember is the day The Mystery Train caught us by surprise and left us feeling foolish and cheated. At least I think that's what the grown ups felt, us youngsters didn't care, we had a great time.

We did all the usual things the night before, eggs, tomatoes, onions were everywhere and the sliced pan wrappers all packed up before we went to bed, giving the tomato sandwiches plenty of time to soak overnight, in time for an early start in the morning. All ready after a quick wash we set off with bags and baggage walking down the lane known as The Metals to the local train station, the cousins and friends swinging the food bags and singing – " We, don't know where we're goin' ". All piled on to the local train, filling two compartments with the lovely old slidey - down windows and the big leather straps to let them up and down. We kept the windows open a bit so that we could all smell the smoke as the train passed under bridges and tunnels. This train was a " Billy – Puffer " 'cos the smoke was black, the trains with the white smoke were ' Sammy Steams '. Arriving in Amiens Street Station we got on the Mystery Train and waited in eager anticipation. The train filled up with families from all over Dublin, singing and shouting in a mixture of Dublin accents, until a big cheer followed our train whistle blowing, as we started to move and the Mystery Train Trip had begun.

Off we went looking and wondering where we were going, until we thought "this is odd". The Mystery Train was moving back the same way we had come into Dublin, and pretty soon we were passing quickly through Glasthule where we had started our journey that morning. We kept going thinking we were off to Wexford and the Sunny Southeast which wouldn't be too bad. Next station we passed was Glenageary, then Dalkey, Killiney, and Bray, where the train stopped. *"Bray? We can't be going to Bray "*. But we were. The grown ups in our crowd and others who were neighbours looked at each other, and laughed, eventually. Still, Bray was great, we made our way to the sandy seafront in front of the amusement arcades and settled down on the grass at the bandstand. A day filled with paddling, splashing and catching crabs gave us huge appetites for soggy sandwiches so wet you could nearly drink them. Tea was made and drunk, and the men went over the road for a pint while the women talked and kept peace among the squabbling children. Eventually it was time to go. Back up along Albert Walk past a row of chip shops with great smells. Faces and fingers were sticky with candyfloss, stingy with salt and vinegar, and sore with sand. And the sand was everywhere, in knickers, shoes, socks and slips, stuck to us every sorry step home. At Bray station while we waited for the train to go we did what we always did at Bray station, go to the big metal stamp machine at the front door. Once you put in your sixpence you moved a big heavy hand like the hand of a clock to point at each letter in your name. After each letter you pulled an even bigger heavier handle to punch the letter, and at the end out fell a shiny metal bracelet with your name punched in raised letters. Bray was the only place with one of these great machines and you treasured the punched bracelet, until you lost it.

The Mystery Train this time had one last surprise. The train moved off, and kept going, racing swiftly through all the stations including Glasthule which was our home and took us all back to Amiens Street. There we had to wait to get another train to go back to Glasthule, home and a sandy scratchy bed.

Someone, must've been a grown up, said "I never want to see another train as long as I live", but they didn't mean it.

Kathleen, Ann and May in Kilkenny.
This picture taken beside the river in Kilkenny where we had all travelled to on one of the Mystery Train Tours.

A Bit of Omerta. A Good Bit.

Naturally having learned the news from Kathleen at the Tea in the Burlington, and the news I learned from Birth Certificates and the Adoption Certificate, I needed to know more about Kathleen and the time she had the baby, me.

I tried to talk about it with Kathleen herself when I visited her in Donnybrook Hospital, but she didn't want to talk or tell me more than she had already said. She was so vehement and upset when I tried to raise the subject that I did not push her to tell me more. I began to suspect that there was a lot more to be learned and that her reluctance to tell me more, was in a sense to protect me from some elements of the story, for my own good. I was right in this line of thinking, but I did not learn the truth of it for many years after Kathleen had passed away.

I regretted afterwards that I did not try harder, even at the risk of upsetting her. Perhaps I should have asked Jacinta to talk to Kathleen on her own without me, perhaps Kathleen might have spoken more openly with Jacinta, woman to woman, even if she had to swear Jacinta to secrecy for years.

So with the pieces I did know about, I started to talk to family, to relatives who knew Kathleen when I was born, with very mixed and disappointing results. One of the better sources of information was Deirdre (Dee) Butler. Deirdre was the eldest daughter of Ina and Eddie Butler. Ina and Kathleen were cousins, and Ina lived at 23 Findlater Street, across the road

Photograph of Kathleen with Deirdre Butler, aged around 6, eldest daughter of Ina Butler, first cousin of Kathleen, and also friend of Francie Byrne. This picture taken around 1948/9 at the top of Findlater Street where both Ina and Kathleen lived. We spent years trying to work out if Kathleen was wearing an engagement ring in the picture, and whose ring it might be.

from Kathleen in number 19. They were very close friends. It was through Deirdre that another part of the story began to come together. Deirdre was born in 1943 and her father Eddie was in the British Army and away for the duration of the war, mostly in North Africa. Before, during and after the war there was another relative on the scene in Glasthule, his name was Francie. His family were related to the Swords and he and his wife Edith lived on Eden Road near Findlater Street. They had no children and Edith, his wife, was a bit strange. In those straightened times when families had very little, Francie, who was an agent for the Irish Hospitals Sweepstake tickets, was a flamboyant and a colourful character, he seemed to have money where many others had very little. He befriended both Ina and Kathleen, his cousins who both found him exciting in these dull times. He was taking Ina and Kathleen out, sometimes together, for walks, drinks or dances. In fact Deirdre tells the story that when her father Eddie returned unannounced after the war, and approached her as a little girl sitting on the doorstep of her home, she didn't know him. 'Is your mammy in the house? ' he asked her. 'Yes', she said, 'she's going out'. It seems that Ina was inside getting ready to go out, with Francie. Eddie put an end to that.

Deirdre and a few others I spoke to who were very close to Kathleen around 1950 felt sure that Francie Byrne, Kathleen's cousin, was my biological father. Kathleen became pregnant around March 1950 though it was never fully confirmed or

*Francie Byrne, a handsome man.
It's no wonder Kathleen fell for him.*

explained as to the circumstances.

It is noteworthy and typical of Ina, as we learnt many years later, that when Kathleen was pregnant and unmarried Ina offered to take the baby and rear it as one of her own. God love Ina, she had a large family of her own and a small house in which to rear them. She felt she had so many problems and so much on her plate, that a little more would make no difference. So as a result of these conversations with Deirdre and others, we began to close in on our inquiries on Francie Byrne, Kathleen's first cousin, but we had no idea where he went after he left Ireland in 1951, less than one year after I was born. The hunt for Francie and his progress after he left Ireland would be long and complicated before we produced any results. Meanwhile I continued to talk to close family and friends of Kathleen, expecting great information to come quickly and easily. I couldn't have been more wrong. It was exasperating and frustrating. Some of the relatives I spoke to on my own, in other meetings I had my cousin John with me as I began not to trust my recollections of what was being said in detail, and also to observe the chemistry of such meetings and conversations. They all remembered and fondly recalled memories of Aunt Kathleen, and the times they spent with her. But of the time when Kathleen was pregnant with me and the time of my birth, almost nothing was recalled, or at least always almost nothing was passed on to me. I found it frustrating and perplexing – how could these family and friends, who knew and loved Kathleen so well, not recall anything of her unmarried pregnancy and of giving birth to me. They knew alright – I knew that they knew more, I could sense it. But they weren't saying anything to me about it now, over forty years later. They must have known a lot more but they weren't saying anything to me in particular either to protect my feelings or out of some powerful family 'Omerta' to which they had been committed, way back in the 50s.

There was one close relative, very close, and a named part of this story, who had been very helpful to Kathleen at the time. When I spoke to him seeking information which I suspected he must surely have, he said he knew little or nothing, claiming he was out at work all the time and not party to the conversations among the women, that times were very different then and now. I'm not suggesting there was anything malicious in his not telling me what he knew, this was a generous man who would give you the shirt off his back, but this was different, this was not for telling, at least not to me.

And yet I discovered that this man had been able to tell one of his daughters about me being Kathleen's Child, and the father being 'some fella from England who Kathleen was seeing'. This conversation had occurred many years before my conversation with Kathleen over Tea in the Burlington. It seems a lot of people knew a lot about it, long before I did, but no one was saying.

The enquiries continued in this vein, usually getting nowhere, until I met Marina.

*Kathleen at work in the Lee Dairy,
Dún Laoghaire 1938.*

A Bit of a Dip into the Diddley
1954 and 1998

Aunt Kathleen had worked in a number of different jobs before and after I was born in 1950. Typically they were jobs in catering or retail; she had worked at one time in McGovern's shop near the People's Park in Dun Laoghaire. McGovern's were famous in Dun Laoghaire as shops selling grocery, vegetables, dairy, and tobacco products. Kathleen's sister Annie had also worked in McGovern's for years.

After I was born and settled Kathleen had to get back into work to support herself and others. After a few different jobs she worked in 1953/54 in Langan's Post Office and shop in Sallynoggin where she worked closely with her friend Marina. She was great friends with Marina Hayden, with Marina's brother Archie, and with Marina's mother Charlotte. Times were tough then and no one, at least not in Kathleen's circle, were well off. With no qualifications and limited experience she was lucky to get a job in retail, although these shop jobs did not pay very well. To help with unexpected events or expenses Kathleen, Marina, their friend Mary Hughes, and others in the post office ran a small casual savings scheme among themselves which they called 'The Diddly', the name based on the phrase diddly-squat, meaning very little or almost nothing. The scheme was like an early form of Credit Union, they each made regular small donations or lodgements, and took turns by rotation to be able to make a withdrawal.

One day Kathleen came to Marina in an awful state of upset, crying her eyes out. She explained to Marina that although she knew it was not her turn to withdraw from the Diddley, something had cropped up and she had to get money from somewhere, quickly. She explained to Marina that it was to do with the baby, Martin. The baby was being raised by Kathleen's brother Pat and his wife May, in an informal adoption. Now that new adoption legislation had been introduced in 1953, the baby was to be formally adopted by Pat and May. But this was not possible while a full Birth Certificate existed, naming a living married mother, Kathleen Burke, and an apparently living father, Thomas Burke, for the baby, Martin Mary Burke. Kathleen explained to Marina that this first Birth Certificate was made up by Kathleen, with a false married name, false father's name, and false address, 29 Corrig Avenue, when in fact the baby's father was Kathleen's first cousin from England. She explained that now she had to go to a commissioner for oaths and swear that the first Birth Certificate information was all false, and arrange for a new correct Birth Certificate to be issued, to allow the formal adoption to proceed. I don't know how much money was needed for this fee, but she needed it fast. She got the money from Marina. The appointment with the Commissioner was kept. And the corrected Birth Certificate was issued by The Registrar of Births, Deaths and Marriages.

As a result the formal adoption of the baby now called Martin Mary Swords could proceed.

The significance of this incident is that during my enquiries about Kathleen from family, friends, and acquaintances, this was the first instance recorded of Kathleen actually saying the words that my biological father was her 'cousin from England'. This was Francie Byrne. That this conversation happened in 1954, four years after I was born, under circumstances of duress, may have caused her to drop her guard in what she said to Marina. When you're chasing down family history you never know what you're going to hear, and from whom.

Marina and Kathleen.
photograhed many years after the 'diddley'.

A Bit Sick on the Bus. Again.

When I was young, six to eight, I was sick a lot. I don't mean sickly, poorly, or confined to bed. No, I mean physically sick, throwing up. This happened often and was triggered by the simplest and most unexpected things. Perhaps from an unpleasant smell, I would throw up. If I stood on a worm or a snail, I would throw up immediately on the spot. I remember Kathleen and May saying that I had a nervous tummy, whatever that was.
But it happened often, and regularly on the bus.
We traveled often by bus, people like us didn't have cars. I was usually travelling with Ma. Getting the bus at the bottom of Booterstown Avenue for a journey along the Rock Road to Blackrock or Dun Laoghaire, or further afield to Merrion or Sandymount if Ma was going on one of her cleaning jobs, and had to take me along.
I didn't travel well, some combination of my nervous tummy, motion sickness, and often the strong vibrations of the bus, and the strong smell of diesel fumes, regularly made me sick while on the bus. If we made the mistake of sitting too far up the bus, maybe because it was full, then if I got sick on the bus floor, there was a major problem. This was a time when there were two men, always men, working on each bus. The driver in his cab was separated from the passengers. Inside the bus the

conductor was in charge. He was ringing the bell to stop and go, collecting fares upstairs and downstairs, and generally in control of public behaviour on the bus such as smoking, upstairs only. So when I got sick on the floor downstairs, it was a big problem and the conductor took charge. There was no question of his cleaning up, it was not his job to do that. There was nothing for it but to stop the bus at the next stop and ask all the passengers to leave the bus and wait for the next bus to arrive. There was a lot of grumbling and giving out among the passengers and 'dagger's looks' directed towards Ma and me.

I was too young and unwell to be embarrassed at this, but Ma did not know where to look. Ma and I stood at the bus stop where we were put off, with all the other disgruntled passengers. She usually did not stay at the stop very long, but walked away with me to some other bus stop. She said it was to give me air, but really it was all too embarrassing for her. Probably the driver and conductor were more pleased than vexed at this unscheduled return to the bus depot where the bus could be cleaned.

We learned that it was better if there was a seat near the entrance platform, to sit there as there was more breeze and fresh air at that end of the bus. But there was no guarantee I wouldn't be sick again. There was no door on the bus but there was an entrance platform with a metal pole from floor to ceiling where passengers got on and off.

Some of the conductors got to know us from previous journeys, some of them had had to stop and empty buses as a result of my nervous tummy, and were often expecting the worst when they saw us. Some were cross and grumpy, others were nice, kind and helpful. But I was still getting sick.

Sometimes when I felt sick sitting at the back rather than the front of the bus, I was brought by the conductor or Ma, or both, to stand at the entrance platform, holding tightly on to the pole, while getting sick out onto the road as the bus sped along. Health and Safety considerations, to say nothing of Political Correctness issues, hardly existed then and after I was sick things settled down, sort of. At least the bus was not stopped and emptied of passengers. It would not have looked very good to walkers on the pavement, or cyclists or car drivers driving on the road beside the bus, to watch me puking as the bus drove along the road. But people were very understanding and maybe some of them got sick too occasionally.

Eventually I grew out of this condition, just as well, as I would soon be travelling by bus from Dun Laoghaire to Stillorgan to school, on my own. Some of the conductors would remember me from my earlier episodes on the bus, standing on the back platform along the Rock Road.

I wondered much much later when I knew fully about my background, what had contributed to this nervous tummy phenomenon. There may have been a simple explanation, people after all always suffer from travel sickness, particularly those without cars. But I also began to suspect that these nervous feelings were somehow connected in some way to much earlier feelings of anxiety, nervousness, isolation or abandonment, associated with my time spent in Temple Hill Orphanage with St Patrick's Guild. It's impossible at this remove in time to really know what I felt way back then but you never know, nothing about this story surprises me anymore.

I guess I really was a good boy.
On a family trip to the beach,
either Killiney or Bray.

A Bit of a Struggle with Saint Patrick's Guild

1995

Following on from learning the news of my being Kathleen's Child and being formally adopted by Mary and Pat Swords, Kathleen's brother and his wife, I continued enquiries within the family, with mixed results. It had been clear from the Birth Certificates and the Adoption Certificate what had happened. Kathleen had created a false Birth Certificate for me, with the best of intentions, but this had had to be legally corrected in 1954 to facilitate my formal adoption.

From the little bits of good information I was getting from some family members we had established two important things. Firstly, that my birth and coming home to Kathleen's sister's address, to Annie and Jim Goggins, and their son John, on Corrig Avenue, was very stressful on all involved. (Kathleen was not allowed to go home with the baby to her own home, to live with her mother Ellen.) So quickly, over 4 months, Kathleen was persuaded to place the baby for adoption in St Patrick's Guild Temple Hill Blackrock. She was not happy about this at all. In order to find out more I would have to start talking to St Patrick's Guild, now in 1995, about records and events from 1951, if they still had them. They had. I'll give the nuns great credit for record keeping.

Secondly it appeared from first and second hand reports and circumstantial evidence that the most likely candidate for my biological father was Francis Sidney Byrne, Kathleen's first cousin who was very much on the scene in all of 1950.

Both areas needed further investigation, something that would keep me and friends and family busy for years, in fact we're still not finished.
Where to start? I started with the nuns and St Patrick's Guild, SPG.
I called into the SPG office at 82 Haddington Road in Dublin to check I was dealing with the right office and to get a name to write to.
I was advised to write to Sister Gabriel Murphy, so I did, in late 1995. I got no reply. I then got to speak to her and arranged to drop in to talk to her, which I did. She told me there was no file on my name.
I wrote again giving her the benefit of the doubt as it struck me I might not be filed there as Martin Mary Swords but as Martin Mary Burke, the name on my first Birth Certificate. (I was right as it happened, but I would not discover this was the case until much later). I got nothing further from sister Gabriel, apart from a general canvassing leaflet looking for donations to SPG.
I wrote again to sister Gabriel, but heard no more.

Many years later, when I knew much more about my story, I learned from a Facebook Page associated with former children of Temple Hill / SPG, among the many harrowing stories from people's interactions with SPG, that many people had had a very hard experience of dealing with sister Gabriel. I was lucky. I was only ignored, but many others were misled and refused help with information. Many were made to feel as worthless as their own mother's were made to feel back when they had their babies.

I should have followed up quickly but as ever I was busy being busy, and got distracted.

In 1998 I got annoyed with the situation, and with myself. I was there, and therefore there must be a record of my stay. I decided a charm offensive was called for. I wrote them a cheque and sent it.

In January 1998 I received a letter from Sister Francis Ignatius Fahy (see appendix)
…….. thank you for your generous donation of £25 to St Patrick's Guild. Sister Gabriel Murphy retired at the end of last February……. I have checked and located your records here.

So there was a record of my file and Sister Fahy shared some of it with me when I called in and met her.

There was an application for baby Martin Mary Burke to be admitted to SPG / Temple Hill, admitted 17th April 1951.

Kathleen is named on the application as Kathleen Swords (Mrs. Burke) aged 32, recommended by Mrs. Goggins (sister). A putative father was named, and address given. The fee mentioned was £70 for adoption. The remarks mentioned Kathleen's 'father dead, mother alive and aware'. Also on the file was my incorrect Birth Certificate and my incorrect Baptism Certificate where I was baptized as Martin Mary Burke, born December 9th 1950, baptised 13th day of December, witnessed by James Goggins and Annie Goggins. (Incidentally I have never been baptised with my correct name Martin Mary Swords – I'm sure God understands.)
There was also on the file a copy of the agreement for placing me into the care of St Patrick's Guild of 50 middle Abbey Street Dublin to start the 17th day of April 1951 with a monthly fee of £2 for maintenance. The agreement was signed and cross witnessed by Kathleen Burke and Mrs. A Goggins. Alongside this was a copy of a Certificate of Surrender signed by Kathleen Burke………. *"handed over my child Martin Mary…... to the custody of St Patrick's Guild….. I surrender him completely and entirely"*. Heartbreaking.

I was surprised to see on the file two handwritten letters from Mrs Annie Goggins, April 14th 1951, and July 27th 1951, to Sister Frances Elizabeth, the Sister-in-Charge in Temple Hill. The letters from Annie, which were not to be shown to Kathleen, indicate that Annie was helping Kathleen to solve the situation, even if it was not to be solved the way Kathleen would prefer. The letters, in full in the appendix, show how central Annie was, and give some indication of the stress that was occurring with Annie and Jim in their flat on 29 Corrig Avenue Dun Laoghaire, as caretakers of the Dun Laoghaire Bridge Club, with their young 10-month old son John. Jim, it seems, was not asked about taking in Kathleen and me, and they were very much afraid of losing their jobs and the accommodation by taking in a lodger, even a close relative. The letters indicate the urgency of Baby Burke, me, being placed in Temple Hill and adopted as quickly as possible so everything could get back to normal. But Kathleen had other ideas and was working steadily to come up with her own solution, which she eventually did.

It is worth noting that when I got more from my file years later, I saw that Mrs Annie Goggins paid the first £2 monthly maintenance fee for Kathleen on the 18th of April 1951, the day after I was surrendered. Thank You Aunt Annie. It is curious to read Annie's letters to St. Patrick's Guild, Temple Hill, and to get a sense of what was being expected, it was Annie's expectation that the adoption of Martin Mary would happen quickly, and that would be good, and all would be well. One small thing in the files did strike me forcefully as being of those times and those circumstances. In a few places Kathleen is referred to as 'the girl', which seems very impersonal and demeaning. Still, in 1950-51, if you were a 'fallen woman', you stayed fallen and there was no longer any need to extend kindness, courtesy and dignity to 'the girl', even if she is thirty two years old.

So from around 1994/95 I had been dealing with Saint Patrick's Guild and looking for access to more from my files. Firstly, with no results dealing with Sister Gabriel Murphy with whom I sensed I was not welcome, and no great effort made to be helpful to me enquiring into such an odious subject.

From 1998 onwards I was in regular contact with Sister Francis Fahy whom I found to be very helpful, kind, courteous and efficient. Thank You Sister Fahy. I got a lot of the material from my file from her, and after that I kept on corresponding with her and informing her of new developments, such as my meeting and conversation with Marina. Sister Fahy thought this meeting was hugely important, as did I, and she confirmed that in family situations like this 'the information which you have obtained is of the kind that only family members know. It is quite amazing how much information is retained within the wider family circle, if one puts the right question to the right person!'

Sister Fahy did provide me with much that was on my file in St Patrick's Guild, and went further, writing to the National Maternity Hospital, Holles Street and the Adoption Board on my behalf, to seek any further records they might have on my birth and adoption in December 1950 and in 1954, both sources providing interesting information which I might not have gotten on my own.

And yet, and yet, all this fascinating material was 'big stuff' from the files. I remained convinced that there must be more material on the file, material that might be regarded by some as 'small stuff', thought to be of little interest. Yet to the baby in question searching for his past such material was very important, personal and touching. It might be a baby name tag or a receipt signed by a mother. Throwaway stuff, yet vitally important. I knew there must be more small stuff on the file, and I was right. But I would not get to this material until I had locked horns with TUSLA. Dealing with St Patrick's Guild was a walk in the park compared to dealing with the legal and bureaucratic mindset in TUSLA who had taken over the control and management of all of St Patrick's Guild files in 2016.

St. Patrick's Guild, Temple Hill, Blackrock.

ADOPTION

LOVELY BOY

two years of age for Adoption. For particulars apply to

THE SISTER IN CHARGE, ST. PATRICK'S GUILD, 50, Middle Abbey Street Dublin

For Adoption
LOVELY BOY
2 YEARS OF AGE
For particulars apply to:
SISTER IN CHARGE
St. Patrick's Guild,
50 Middle Abbey St.,
Dublin 1

NOTICES.
WILL childless couple adopt Finbarr? Aged 2 years 2 months, healthy little boy, fair, very intelligent, happy disposition; full surrender; no fee; home must be well recommended; priest's reference essential. For particulars apply Sister in Charge, St. Patrick's Guild, 50 Middle Abbey Street, Dublin.

Old newspaper advertisements from the 1950s and 1960s looking for couples to adopt babies and young children. The advertisements appeared in Dublin and Cork newspapers.

How much for THE LOVELY BOY?

Another Bit of a Struggle, this time with TUSLA, and a Bit of a Breakthrough.
2018

I first made contact with TUSLA in June 2018. This was a few years after all of the controversy of TUSLA taking over all of the files of Saint Patrick's Guild (SPG). There was a great deal of comment in the media about SPG going into liquidation, the files being 'saved' by TUSLA, but being 'sealed' from the public for seventy-five years. This move was also connected to the breaking scandal of the Mother and Baby Homes and the discovery by historian Catherine Corless of the burial over time of up to eight hundred infants, in what may have been once a septic tank, in the grounds of the Mother and Baby Home in Tuam. Other news of other burials broke in many other Mother and Baby Homes around the country. The shocked reaction to all this news and the changing attitude and outcry against nuns, clergy, and County Councils, or anyone who knew of and covered up the secret scandal of the last eighty years, was huge. Thousands of mother's, babies and family of those possibly buried in these often unmarked and hidden, 'Angel Plot' graves, were clamouring for assistance in exhumations, DNA identification, and accountability in this growing scandal. This was as bad the previous scandals of sexual abuse by priests in schools, reformatories and industrial schools. This was as bad only this time with the nuns, no doubt assisted by parish priests who often started the process of referring the unmarried mothers to the nuns to have their babies in Mother and Baby Homes. From which homes such babies might be adopted, often overseas, for considerable fees, to 'good Catholic homes'. But the infant mortality rate in these places was high, unusually high, and there were rumours of neglect or lack of urgent care, perhaps especially among the weak and sickly ones unlikely to be adopted.

The scandal continues to this day, with difficulty, and with very little accountability or explanation. Against all this background I thought again about the information I had gotten from St Patrick's Guild. I had been delighted to get the information I had so far, but remained sure in my mind that there was more to be gleaned from the files.
And now that TUSLA had taken over all the files, I thought I would approach them for sight of my files.
I had no idea what I was starting.
My dealings with TUSLA were eventually very good, but I was not ready for the level of bureaucracy and legal considerations I would run into.
With the assistance of all that I had learned from SPG, file reference numbers and the fact that my previous search had overcome the confusion at the start of my search involving my name being both Martin Swords and Martin Burke, and that my mother's name had been first Kathleen Burke and then Kathleen Swords, my file was located by TUSLA and forwarded to me. To my delight my file was more complete than

that which I had seen from St Patrick's Guild. Yes, it contained all that I had seen from SPG, and a great deal more besides. And that 'great deal more besides', really mattered to me, because it contained a lot of the small stuff which I suspected might be there, receipts for payments by Kathleen, and notes from Kathleen to SPG about 'Baby Burke', all of which was treasure to me. I will tell you about the treasure shortly but I was shocked to see that in the file from TUSLA there were a great many pages that were redacted or blanked out, with no clue as to why they were redacted or what they may have been about. Getting the redacted pages released to me was more complicated and took much longer to resolve than getting all the other information that was on my file. The executives I dealt with in TUSLA were very kind, particularly a lady called Maria Brown, Freedom of Information Decision Maker, who was very helpful and patiently explained to me that the holding back of certain pages had to do with protecting the privacy of the third parties involved, even where that third party was deceased.
In fact, although it seems ridiculous one of those third parties whose privacy must be protected was Kathleen Swords herself, my mother, already deceased. I actually had to get and provide a solicitor's affidavit to state that I was who I was, the next of kin of the late Kathleen Swords, and supply a copy of Kathleen's death certificate. This then released a small two inch piece of paper written by the Assistant Master of Holles Street National Maternity Hospital, dated the 14th of the 4th 1951, stating that Mrs. Burke's test for WR is negative. In other

words, Kathleen Burke did not have syphilis when I was born. For other redacted pages I had to lodge an appeal to higher management in TUSLA to review decisions made to withhold information, the reviews were inevitably upheld and the pages stayed redacted.

In other instances material was redacted because it had to do with my adoption and needed to be appealed to the Adoption Board. I could not appeal to the Adoption Board because I was only an 'adoptee' and not an 'adoptor', and the adoptors were deceased. Catch-22.

A possible route to resolutions was to appeal to the Office of the Information Commissioner to review the decisions made by TUSLA following my Freedom of Information request for my full file. I received back detailed reviews and legal opinion which I couldn't understand, or which seemed more appropriate to espionage or subversion of the constitution. In any case nothing more was released. In fact as I write in 2021 there are still enquiries unresolved.

But on to happier things, the new material I got from TUSLA, what I call the small stuff, was wonderful and heartwarming.

It included a series of receipts for payments made by Kathleen to SPG

'Enclosed £2 being payment for Martin M Burke for coming month'.
Kathleen Swords

At some point Kathleen stopped calling herself Kathleen Burke in correspondence, even though I was still named as Martin M Burke

The first of these receipts dated 18th of April 1951 was from Mrs. Goggins for Martin M Burke', indicating that Kathleen's sister Annie had paid the first payment for Kathleen.

A small note from Dr Evelyn Nixon, 'Casa Loma', Dun Laoghaire stating that...
'Baby Martin Burke (3 months) had been examined by me today. He is healthy and free from infectious diseases.
12th April 1951

A note to Miss Kathleen Swords, a receipt for payment, asking *if receipts are to be kept in SPG office.*

All good wishes

Yours Sincerely in J.C.
(Sister in charge)

A small note from SPG, two copies of the Certificate of

Surrender both signed, one signed Kathleen Swords the other signed Kathleen Burke, both dated 14-4-'51, both different, both struck through with a line and both written with handwritten notes (different)
'Cancelled per telephone call 19-7-'51.'

There must have been two Certificates of Surrender, different names.

A note from Sister-in-Charge to Mrs. Annie Goggins in response to one of Annie's letters to SPG
'……..We will have a little talk with Kathleen. Do not be worrying….. fond of the child... but with God's grace she will act wisely concerning it.'
                                                  30 July 1951

Small note…... enclosed £2 pounds…….
... 6th September 1951
K. Swords

Handwritten by SPG, 'this child is not for adoption, going home in two months about'

Kathleen's plans must have been well in train at this stage.

Small note from K. Swords
'enclosed £2 being payment for Martin M Burke up to October 30th on

which day I will take him from the home'
                              K Swords

Small letter from K. Swords   23-11-'51

    Dear Sister Francis Elizabeth,

……….. Baby Burke….. he settled into his new home at once and is quite happy there. They are all delighted with him…..

Thanking you very much for all you have done for me.
I remain yours faithfully
                              K. Swords

Small letter from Sister-in-Charge to Miss K Swords

    '*Dear Miss Swords*
            …... glad to know little Baby Burke is so well and so settled down. I am sending you his ration book…..
        …….. yours sincerely in JC.

From confidential file note from SPG on child.
Child's name;   Burke, Martin Mary,   No. 4501

        'Discharged to Mother   30/10/1951

This was all the small stuff from the file that I suspected might be there. Little Treasures every one.

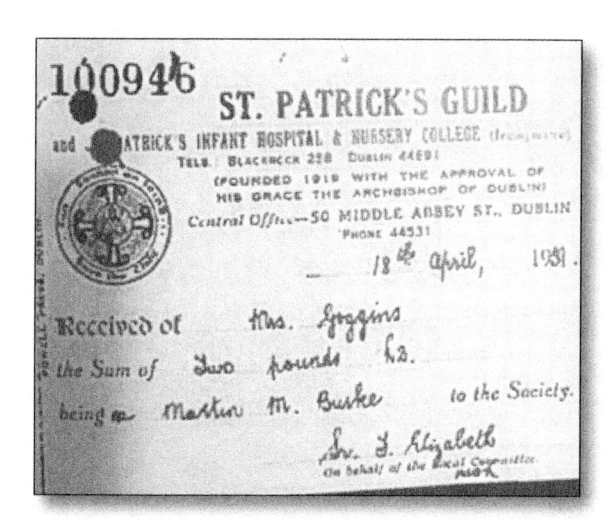

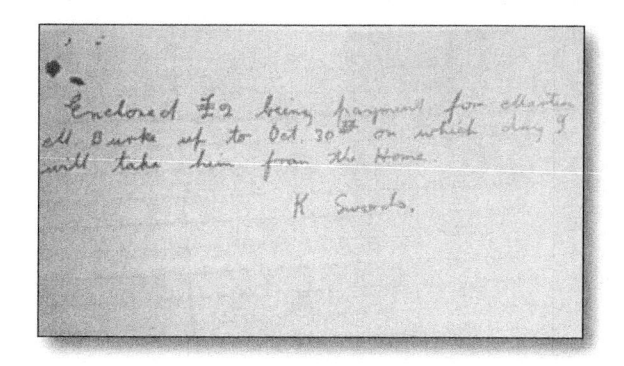

Receipts to Kathleen from St. Patrick's Guild

204

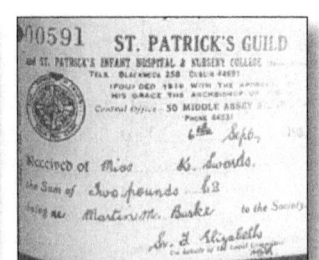

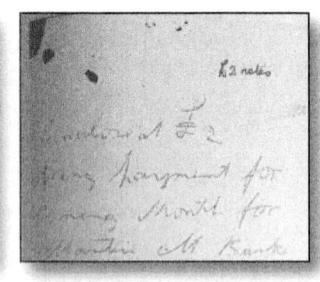

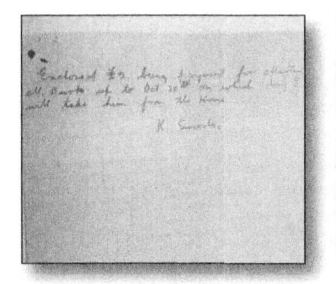

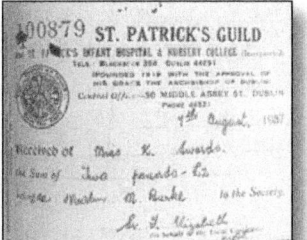

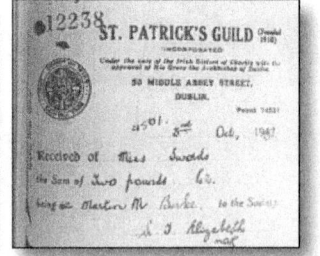

Public Bodies - AAI Not Covered

An Bord Uchtála　　　　　　　　　　　Adoption Board
Teach Shelbourne　　　　　　　　　　Shelbourne House,
Bóthar Shelbourne,　　　　　　　　　Shelbourne Road,
Droichead na Dothra,　　　　　　　　Ballsbridge,
Baile Átha Cliath 4　　　　　　　　　　Dublin 4.

A172/54

Tel: (01) 667 1392
Fax: (01) 667 1438

8 September 1998

Private & Confidential

Sr Francis Ignatius Fahy
St Patrick's Guild
82 Haddington Road
Dublin 4

Re: Tracing Request - Martin Swords, d.o.b. 9/12/50

Dear Sr Francis

Your enquiry of the 11th August re. the above-named has been allocated to me.

I have checked the records held by the Board and I hope the following will be of assistance to you in helping Mr Swords with his enquiries. This information is provided on the usual non disclosure basis.

Child: Martin Mary Swords, d.o.b. 9/12/50
Birth mother: Kathleen Swords, d.o.b. 25/2/18. She signed the consent to adoption 13/4/54 and her address at that time was 29 Corrig Avenue, Dun Laoghaire.

The application for an adoption order was made by Patrick Swords, described as uncle to the child and Mary Swords, described as aunt by marriage. The adoption order was made 22/11/54 and the address of the adopters at that time was shown as 7 Pembroke Terrace, Booterstown, Co Dublin.

I trust the above information will be of assistance and should you wish to contact me please do not hesitate to do so.

Yours sincerely

Heather Houston
Social Worker

HH-Lts-9Sep

Public Bodies - AAI Not Covered   13 AU 1998

An Bord Uchtála
Teach Shelbourne,
Bóthar Shelbourne,
Droichead na Dothra,
Baile Átha Cliath 4

Adoption Board
Shelbourne House,
Shelbourne Road,
Ballsbridge,
Dublin 4.

Reference No: A172/54
Your Reference:

Tel: (01) 667 1392
Fax: (01) 667 1438

12/8/98

Re: Martin Swords born 9/12/50
adopted by
Patrick + Mary Swords,
7 Pembroke Terrace, Booterstown, Co Dublin

Dear Sir Francis

I acknowledge receipt of your communication of 11th August 1998 which is receiving attention.

Yours Sincerely

Geraldine Browne
REGISTRAR

Documents received:
Letter of 11/8/98

REDACTED

A Bit of a Chase Around the World After Francis Sydney Byrne
1987 On

Well that had been a bit of a struggle. From 1987 up to now, 2021, I had been toing and froing, in and out, pursuing my files between Saint Patrick's Guild and then TUSLA, not to mention the Office of the Information Commissioner and the Adoption Board.

I was lucky, and some of the people I met along the journey were very nice and helpful, even when it was difficult, some of the people mind you, not all of the people. I was lucky in that I got almost all the material from my files there was available to get. There are one or two more bits outstanding still from the Adoption Board involving those people who adopted me, rather than me myself. But I shall keep on pursuing these extra files. As you saw I got almost everything there was, the 'big stuff' and the 'small stuff' with much of the small stuff being more moving and intimate and therefore all the more valuable to me. Still, when you think about it I was pursuing enquiries for over 30 years to get to this point, and still not finished .

And while all of this was going on we were searching for my biological father, Francie Byrne, Kathleen's cousin, all at the same time. Where was he in 1950 when I was born, and in 1951, and afterwards when he apparently disappeared. But we found him after quite a struggle. When I say 'we' I mean mostly

John, my 'pram brother' so to speak, and a few lucky breaks, which I stumbled upon by accident.

John is the genealogist in the family and very good at using the internet in searches for records and Military Histories. It is fascinating how much information can be discovered from the internet and archival records, if you know where to look, and John knew where to look.

To set the scene with Francie Byrne's family, his father was William Byrne, originally from Redcross in County Wicklow, born 1866. He spent most of his life in England, in Hythe in Kent. He was a Master Shoemaker in the British Army, a sergeant in the King's Royal Rifles Corps, seeing service in the Boer War, and he was still in the British Army during WWI. He married Bridget Roche, Irishtown, Wicklow Town and she moved to Kent with William. They had four children, Reginald Byrne (Reggie), William Byrne (Willie), Annie Byrne, Alfred Byrne (Pat), and Francis Byrne (Francie).

On Kathleen's side, her parents were Patrick Swords (Dublin) and Ellen Roche, Irishtown, Wicklow Town, and 19 Findlater Street Glasthule. Ellen Roche and Bridget Roche were sisters, hence Kathleen and Francie were first cousins. Some of the other Roche family lived in Shankill County Dublin and there was a good bit of contact and visiting between the Roches, the Byrnes and the Swords, mostly in Shankill and in Glasthule, and sometimes in Kent. Reggie visited Glasthule and brought

*A family at war. Byrne family group at time of WWI.
Father, 'Pappy', seated, Francie on right, Willie on left.
Family photographs like this were very often taken at the time because
casualties were widespread and expected, and such photographs
might become a means to remember.
As it happened, Francie was wounded at Ypres, and Willie was killed
in action also in Ypres, never recovered.*

Family portrait, Ellen Swords and children. Annie, left. Patrick, standing. Des, baby. Christy, sailor right. Kathleen was not yet born. Ellen was a skilled seamstress for a living and would have made lots of clothes for the family, including the children's clothes shown here.

*A lovely photo of Kathleen, taken in 1932 we think, when she was 14/15.
Lots of the girls had photos like this, and more formal older photographs.
They were kept in the family, in this case in a shoebox, and used to give copies to friends, pen pals, boyfriends and potential husbands.
They were even retouched by the photographer, look at the eyelashes.
Beautiful smile, mind the gap.*

*A glamorous, elegant and sophisticated picture of
Kathleen taken in 1940 when she was all of 22.
I think people then tended to look older than their age.
A photo for penpals, boyfriends and suitors.
Love the earrings.*

Briget and Ellen, with Mollie, at Killiney beach.

his daughter Mollie to visit her relations. Mollie was a real 'girl guide' type, and she and some of the Swords relations took regular trips to Dun Laoghaire and Killiney seaside. As a keen cyclist she took trips throughout County Wicklow and she kept a journal recording it all. At one point in one of her journal copy book entries she recorded the signatures of all the family relations she met in 1946, including Annie Swords and Kathleen Swords. Mollie in later life moved to Canada where she was very happy as a teacher for all her life.

So while I was busy chasing files from Saint Patrick's Guild and TUSLA, John and I were also looking for Francie. John discovered Francie and his wife Edith through diligent searches on the internet, and I found Mollie Byrne in Vancouver British Columbia, through a stroke of luck.

Francie and Edith in 1950/'51 had given their address as Eden Road in Glasthule, coincidentally only around the corner from Findlater Street where Kathleen and Ina lived. John found them from this address on the passenger list for a boat sailing from Southampton to Australia in 1951, they were 'Ten-Pound Poms' taking the assisted passage scheme to attract new citizens from UK and Commonwealth countries to live and work in Australia. John also found them listed on census returns in Australia, and later in New Zealand, where they moved after a few years, and where they made their home. There was no great evidence of Francie working or starting a business in New Zealand. It was said in family speculation that he may have been involved in buying and selling luxury cars such as Mercedes.

Francie Byrne with his Aunt Katie in Woking.
A warm friendly scene.
Possibly a little too friendly.

In the case of my search for Mollie Byrne I was trolling through a lot of social media sites and educational organisations for a woman of that name. I was probably lucky and helped in that her name was spelt Mollie, and not Molly as was more common. Eventually I stumbled across a Mollie Byrne who was joint author of a book called The Estuary Book, a school text and workbook, produced in 1981 by the Western Education Development Group at the University of British Columbia, for the Ministry of Environment. Through this publication I traced Mollie and wrote to the address I found. It was her all right, and after a while she and John and I all wrote to each other quite a lot. Naturally once we had established our story and her story, her childhood memories of visits to Ireland and recalling the family members we knew in common, we found we had exchanged a lot of information.
I did have to ask her quite pointedly what she recalled of Francie and if she knew of his liaison with Kathleen, and my birth. She said she didn't know anything about it. I wonder, and have always felt that she must have known something, but wasn't saying. The nearest she came to the subject was a reference she made in one of her letters that Francie had a reputation in the family circle as being 'a bit of a ladies' man'. I also know that she visited Francie in New Zealand late in both of their lives, which may have had something to do with Wills or Inheritance, who knows. Mollie did inherit Francie's estate when he died in April 1986.
Meanwhile John was making great progress in tracking the life

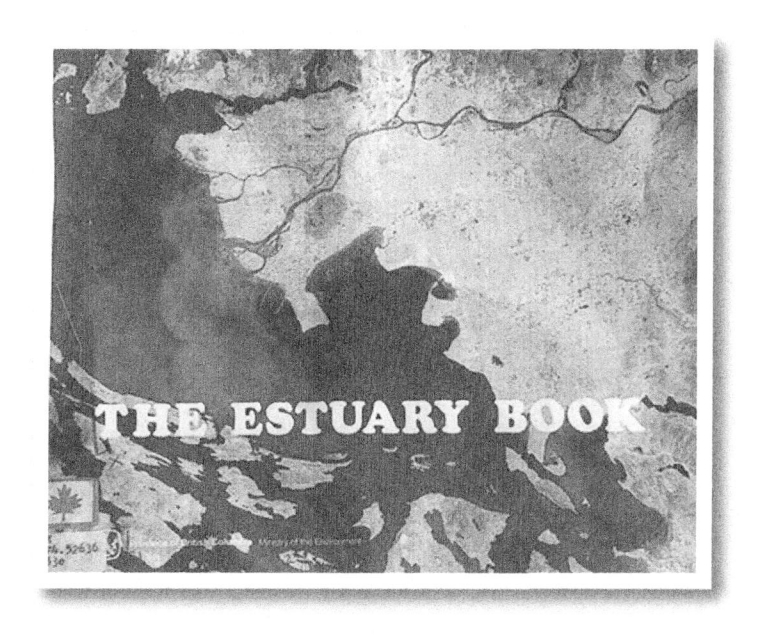

*The Estuary Book, a school textbook produced by
Mollie Byrne while she was teaching.
Discovering this book led us to track down Mollie,
and to making contact and then correspondence.
Important parts of this story.*

of Frances Sydney Byrne. Public access to Wills, Deaths, Burials etc. in New Zealand is very good. He established where Francie lived, and where and when Francie died and was buried, he died in Auckland in 1986 and is buried in Waikumete Cemetery. His wife Edith died two years after Francie, and while we're not sure, we think she suffered poor health and may have been in a public hospital or nursing home suffering from Dementia at the end.

Again through John, who also had a lot of correspondence with Mollie, Mollie passed some of John's correspondence to her sister, or step sister, a lady named Eileen Tuson who was the daughter of Reginald or Reggie Byrne, a brother of Francie's. Eileen lived in Kent, and spent part of the year in Spain. She recalled visits to Ireland with her father and visited places associated with the original family, Waterford, Wicklow, Bray and Shankill, where the home of the family's childhood - 'Clonasleigh'- in Shankill was where Eileen had stayed in 1946, and where some of the Byrnes and Roches lived into old age. The house is demolished and long gone, and only the name survived in the name of a nearby housing estate. Anyway, and very useful for the purposes of this story, Eileen introduced us to Russ Mansfield, a cousin, and son of Marion and Eric Mansfield. His mother, Marion Byrne/Mansfield was the daughter of Alfred Byrne, and a niece of Francie Byrne. Russ and his lovely wife Judy lived in France around this time, 2009. Both Russ and Judy are ex-R.A.F., and Russ has a passion and expertise in Family and Military History. They moved back to the UK soon after, and we made contact with them and started together to trace our joint family history. Russ knew of Francie and his brothers and was familiar with all their Military Histories in W.W.I., and their father's history in the army, including the Boer War and the First World War. Russ didn't know about Francie, Kathleen, and me, that was news to him, but he wasn't surprised given what he had heard of Francie in the past. Russ's wife Judy is an award-winning celebrant and we met them both on a few of their trips to Ireland on duty for celebrant business where we discussed further and explored the complicated family history.

Russ, John, and I, all had DNA tests completed and confirmed. Russ and I are first cousins, confirming our links back to Francie, his brothers and their parents, and John and Russ are second cousins, confirming their links back through the Swords, Byrnes, and Roche's family connections. So things between Francie, Kathleen, me, John and Russ were starting to fix

Russ Mansfield, my newly discovered first cousin and his wife, Judy.

themselves in place. The DNA tests confirmed the close relationships

Russ has a close association with the Commonwealth War Graves Commission and he informed us that the 100th anniversary of the death of Corporal William Byrne, 17th October 1914 in Ypres, was approaching and that we might all like to commemorate this event as 'family' and in a sense on behalf of all the families, the Swords, the Byrnes and Roches. We arranged to travel, John, Russ and I, to Ypres for 27th of October 2014, the anniversary. Russ met us at Birmingham Airport, and we were off to 'Flanders' Fields'. We travelled via the Channel Tunnel to Calais. John and I had not been through the tunnel before and I was fascinated by the fact that sitting in Russ's car we were able to phone Judy from halfway to France using the phone and internet to make the call from deep under the English Channel, with better phone and internet signal than I was used to back in Ireland in County Wicklow. We drove through the beautiful countryside of Northern France and Belgium to arrive in Ypres, now a beautifully restored small town. The history of Ypres, once totally destroyed in W.W.I., was all about the fighting here in the Great War, trenches, destroyed landscapes, and bomb craters. There was an overwhelming sense of the first world war about the town and even though it was now all beautiful with hotels, cafes, museums, and restaurants, I could not escape the feeling that I was in a W.W.I. documentary in black and white. We enjoyed our stay in Ypres, yet it didn't feel like a holiday, being there felt like a solemn duty. We attended the memorial at Menin Gate where we found the name of W. Byrne inscribed with the thousands of other names of those lost and missing, where no body was recovered. Every night at 8 oclock the Last Post is played to the assembled hushed audience in a ceremony that is both dignified and solemn. Russ had been able to arrange for the three of us to present and place a poppy wreath during the Last Post Ceremony on the night of Willie's 100th Anniversary. It was a dignified and solemn colour party ceremony for us three, and very moving. It was Family honouring Family and afterwards it took a long time before we could smile or laugh or talk about anything. It was overwhelming.

Over the next few days we three visited battle sites, the Somme, and the major W.W.I. grave sites such as Tynecot. We saw and read the serried ranks of white headstones, many for unknown soldiers. We found a white headstone for a soldier, unknown, a corporal in the right regiment, The King's Royal Rifle Corps, and the correct date. It could be Willy, unidentified and unknown, it could be. We accepted that maybe it might be, decorated the headstone, took some photographs and said a silent prayer for Family and the Lost.

As well as Willie in W.W.I, Francie, his brother was also wounded in Ypres 1914, but recovered.

It must have been a devastating time for families back home in England and Ireland, and was followed quickly by the Flu Pandemic of 1918, bringing more losses to Irish and English families including our own Swords and Roche families.

We enjoyed our time there, our few beers and meals and our great chat about family history. We visited the magnificent

Poppy wreath i.m. Corporal William Byrne.
'A' Company 1st Battalion King's Royal Rifle Corps.
Born 1893 - KIA 27 October 1914.
First Battle of Ypres, in Flanders Fields.
Wreath presented and laid at The Last Post, Menin Gate,
by Family, 27th October 2014.

*Martin, Russ and John, the wreath laying colour party
at The Last Post, Menin Gate, Ypres, for the 100th Anniversary
of the death of William Byrne.*

Me in the Cathedral in Ypres, now restored having been completely destroyed in WWI in the fighting in and around Ypres. I remember my family talking about this place when I was young, they always called it 'Wipers'.

museum 'In Flanders Fields', in Ypres commemorating all the dead of every side, and we felt a part of European History.
I bought a copy of 'In Flanders Fields' by Herwig Verleyen, the story of Canadian poet John McCrae, author of the famous poem of W.W.I. called 'In Flanders Fields'. I also bought an enamel poppy lapel badge which I wear at home in Ireland, notwithstanding.

And we headed for home. Later at home I finished a poem I had started at the Menin Gate, 'Song for Willie, And Tommy, And Ned'.

While all this was going on, John and I were still searching for anything else we could find out, on official records or unofficial discussions with family members while I was engaged with St Patrick's Guild and later with TUSLA but however, we were making some progress. At one stage because I was working in advertising and media, I placed an advert in the Press in New Zealand looking for information on Francie Byrne. The advert proclaimed 'Desperately Seeking Francie', seeking information about him and suggesting the enquiry was connected to an Estate Legacy, and directing responses to the Legal Department of a company called MSA in Dun Laoghaire. There was no Legal Department, MSA was the name of my Marketing Consultancy, and there were no departments either, only me, a sole trader. I got a few responses but nothing connected to or useful to our search, and a good few offers from Genealogy services in New Zealand looking for business. So much for advertising.

Meanwhile John was doing much better in New Zealand. He was in touch with his equivalent, genealogy enthusiasts there and was directed to the fact that Will's, Probate etc were publicly available once processed. He found Francie's Will and the legal firm that processed it. It recorded Francie's death, on the 26th of April 1986, of Bronchopneumonia and Cerebral Vascular accident and his burial, and it confirmed that he left his estate to his niece Mollie Byrne. But not all of it. Strangely and curiously his will left a sum of $10,000 to 'my friend Mrs Howes, 7 Glen Road, Browns Bay, and her two sons Michael Howes and Peter Howes'. So who was Mrs Howes, and the boys? Naturally, and given Francie's reputation as described by Mollie, we wondered if there had been a relationship between Francie and Mrs Howes. We wondered even if the two boys were Francie's sons, and maybe my half brothers. (Family History and Genealogy is a great area for too easily clutching at straws !). The solicitor knew nothing about the relationship with Mrs Harris, suggesting only that she maybe used to call to see Francie regularly and care for him. Perhaps so. We still try to trace the sons, one now deceased, the other, no luck on Social Media, perhaps he's more interested in his motorbikes, than in family history.

The solicitor was also able to tell us of the death of Francie's wife Edith on 28th July 1988, of Inanition, cremated, Waikumete cemetery. We don't know much about Edith's last year's, we suspect she was unwell for a long time in hospital, not knowing herself or Francie or anything or anyone. Sad.

*Marion Byrne/Mansfield, Russ's mother.
Looking every bit a 'Byrne'.*

*John and Marion.
Being with Marion felt like being in the room with Kathleen*

Back home with Russ and Judy, Russ brought John and I to Galenos House to visit Russ's mum Marion. Galenos House was the Royal British Legion home in Warwickshire, a retirement and nursing home for ex-servicemen and women. Marion was staying there as she was elderly and frail. Russ's dad, Eric Mansfield was also in Galenos House, in a separate room and separate floor, he also was frail and suffering from Dementia. Marion Mansfield, formerly Marion Byrne, was the daughter of Alfred Byrne, a brother of Francie, and therefore a niece of Francie Byrne whom she knew when she was a child. Marion was a lovely lady, a real Byrne and when I met her I thought she had a great look of Kathleen, through the convoluted connections they all had with the Byrne, Swords and Roche families. We chatted away and talked about family history. I explained who I was and told her of the connection between Francie, Kathleen, and me. She understood all that but couldn't confirm the story, she was too young when such a subject might have been alluded to within the extended family, if indeed it ever was referred to at all. I found the meeting with Marion very moving and emotional. Given her strong character and physical family resemblance, I felt with her that it was like being in the room with Kathleen, very moving.

When we left Marion, and were going to the car with Russ, there was the opportunity to visit Russ's father Eric on another floor in Galenos House. We didn't. Russ said Eric would not know us or recognise the names or the family connections, maybe he wouldn't even recognise Russ. We should have gone to see Eric when we had the opportunity, even so, although we were all highly emotional after meeting Marion. I regret ever since that we did not visit Russ's dad at the time. I feel now it was disrespectful to Russ's dad Eric, as family, and it was disrespectful to Russ himself. We got back to Judy who threw her arms around me and I cried, such was the emotion of the meeting with Marion.

Mollie Byrne, Francie's niece, died on the 28th of November 2017, aged 91, in Nanaimo, Vancouver British Columbia, Canada. Apparently Mollie was quite a collector, a hoarder even, of memorabilia, papers, and documents. She still had her photographs and school book journal which she wrote on her visit to Ireland in 1946. She had also acquired photographs and correspondence from Francie's estate in Auckland, on his passing. So all in all there was a lot of memorabilia, and other stuff to be sorted after Mollie's passing. It fell to a combination of Eileen Tuson and Russ and Judy to sort out her affairs and property. Russ arranged that a lot of her photographs and letters were passed on to me and they made for fascinating reading. As well as treasured old photographs of her visits to Ireland and meetings with the older members of the Swords, Byrne, and Roche families, the material recorded the many trips she undertook in Wicklow, and trips to Killiney and Bray for seaside visits and picnics. Many of the photographs recorded meetings with Kathleen, Ina, Annie, Ellen and Katie, photographs we had never seen before. Walks down the East Pier in Dun Laoghaire with the girls and Francie were recalled, indicating that the families and cousins were all close friends back then. Mollie corresponded a lot with Francie in Auckland,

New Zealand and all their letters were there. It was curious to see that in many letters to Mollie, Francie more than a few times encouraged Mollie to 'never get married'. Perhaps his own marriage experience with Edith did not cause him to recommend it, although in the photographs Francie and Edith looked happy enough together, despite a number of relatives commenting that Edith was strange and unwelcoming. Edith seems to have been unwell for a long time towards the end of their lives and gets little mention from Francie in the latter part of his life, she may not even have been with him for a lot of their later life.

Mollie was a niece of Francie, and an aquaintance of all the relatives here in Ireland. She played an important part in this story, once we had found her after much searching.

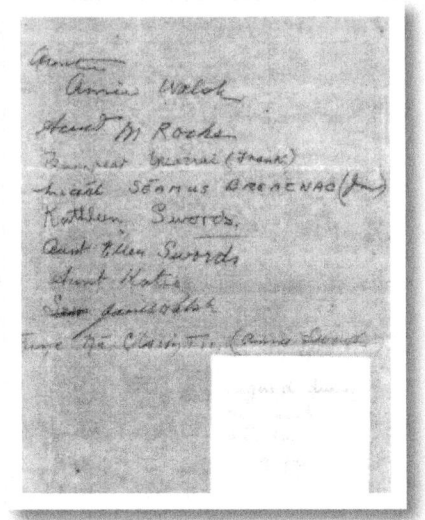

From Mollie's journal, signatures she collected from family on her visit in 1946.

Kathleen as a young girl, maybe thirteen, photographed down the East Pier near the bandstand.
She is standing against the Victorian Chains at the pier edge with one of the old red Lightships, possibly The Kish, in the background moored near the West Pier. This could be on one of the many walks down the pier for Kathleen, Ina, Annie, Francie and Mollie as described by Mollie in her journal about her Irish Holidays.

In looking through all the material that came to me I was disappointed to see that there was no reference to Kathleen by Francie, no photograph being kept as a special keepsake.
I naively thought there might be something, indicating some residue of affection, or even just of remembering, over the years. Clutching at straws again. Perhaps Francie was in a hurry to get away in 1951 and leave Kathleen, me, and the whole episode behind him. Who knows?
Russ and Judy, and Eileen, did a fine job on sorting out the memorabilia, both Mollie's and Francie's, and because Russ had met John and I and knew our story he was particularly attentive to anything in the papers and pictures that might be of interest to me. He brought back a large folder of letters and photographs connected to John and I, pictures of our aunts,

uncles and grandparents we had never seen before, and we treasure them. They included photographs of Francie and friends, and Edith, including pictures on the boat from Southampton when the 'poms' were travelling to Australia. Looking at all the pictures and reading the letters both John and I were struck by a great sense of 'Commonwealth' from those days, this was essentially a group of men and women who were more English than Irish, travelling within their British Commonwealth, to relocate within their Commonwealth Territories, including Mollie's settling in Canada, in British Columbia, as was their right, to live in their own Commonwealth, a residue of the former British Empire. Among the memorabilia were medals belonging to Francie from his time in the King's Royal Rifles Corps, and a beautiful clock. The clock was a beautiful mantel chiming clock, chiming on the quarters and the hours, which had belonged to Pappy, William Byrne, born 1866, died 1937, with an inscribed brass plate mounted on the front.

> To Sergeant W. Byrne
> From Members of Serg'nts Mess
> 3 BT King's Royal Rifles
> On His Leaving the Battn 1909

The Clock had passed down from Pappy, William Byrne, to Francie, to Mollie, and with Russ's help to me.
Russ and Judy had gone to a lot of trouble to save the clock, service and restore it, and to have it
shipped to me. Thank you.

*Grandfather William Byrne, 'Pappy', was presented with this clock by his comrades, of the Sergeant's Mess, when he left The Battalion in 1909.
Now it's happily chiming away in my kitchen.*

Pedigree Chart for Martin Swords

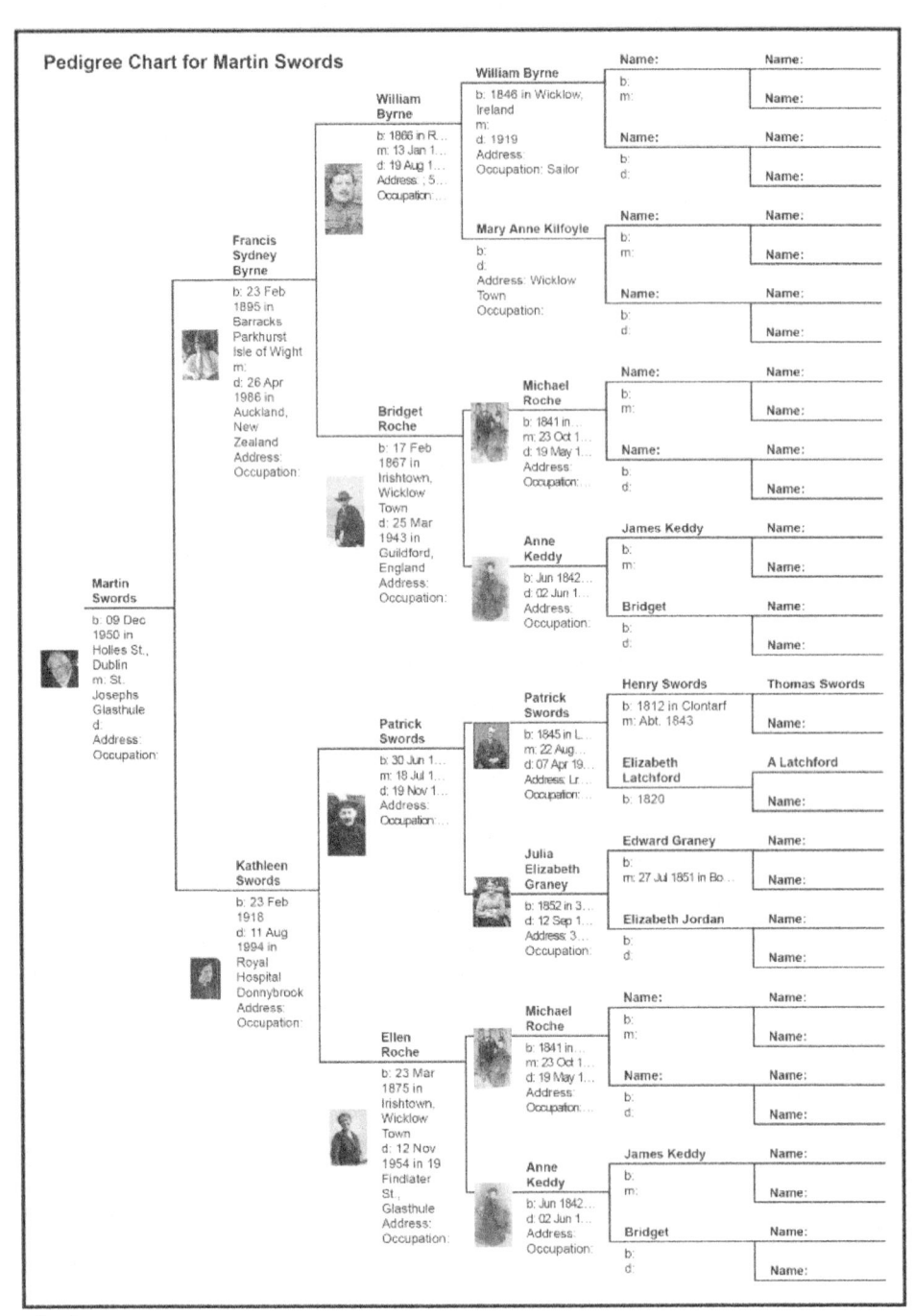

Martin Swords
b: 09 Dec 1950 in Hollies St., Dublin
m: St. Josephs Glasthule
d:
Address:
Occupation:

Father's Line

Francis Sydney Byrne
b: 23 Feb 1895 in Barracks Parkhurst Isle of Wight
m:
d: 26 Apr 1986 in Auckland, New Zealand
Address:
Occupation:

- **William Byrne**
  b: 1866 in R...
  m: 13 Jan 1...
  d: 19 Aug 1...
  Address: ; 5...
  Occupation:

  - **William Byrne**
    b: 1846 in Wicklow, Ireland
    m:
    d: 1919
    Address:
    Occupation: Sailor

  - **Mary Anne Kilfoyle**
    b:
    d:
    Address: Wicklow Town
    Occupation:

- **Bridget Roche**
  b: 17 Feb 1867 in Irishtown, Wicklow Town
  d: 25 Mar 1943 in Guildford, England
  Address:
  Occupation:

  - **Michael Roche**
    b: 1841 in...
    m: 23 Oct 1...
    d: 19 May 1...
    Address:
    Occupation:

  - **Anne Keddy**
    b: Jun 1842...
    d: 02 Jun 1...
    Address:
    Occupation:
    - James Keddy
    - Bridget

Mother's Line

Kathleen Swords
b: 23 Feb 1918
d: 11 Aug 1994 in Royal Hospital Donnybrook
Address:
Occupation:

- **Patrick Swords**
  b: 30 Jun 1...
  m: 18 Jul 1...
  d: 19 Nov 1...
  Address:
  Occupation:

  - **Patrick Swords**
    b: 1845 in L...
    m: 22 Aug...
    d: 07 Apr 19...
    Address: L...
    Occupation:
    - **Henry Swords** b: 1812 in Clontarf m: Abt. 1843
    - **Thomas Swords**

  - **Julia Elizabeth Graney**
    b: 1852 in 3...
    d: 12 Sep 1...
    Address: 3...
    Occupation:
    - **Edward Graney** m: 27 Jul 1851 in Bo...
    - **Elizabeth Jordan**

  - **Elizabeth Latchford** b: 1820
    - **A Latchford**

- **Ellen Roche**
  b: 23 Mar 1875 in Irishtown, Wicklow Town
  d: 12 Nov 1954 in 19 Findlater St., Glasthule
  Address:
  Occupation:

  - **Michael Roche**
    b: 1841 in...
    m: 23 Oct 1...
    d: 19 May 1...
    Address:
    Occupation:

  - **Anne Keddy**
    b: Jun 1842...
    d: 02 Jun 1...
    Address:
    Occupation:
    - James Keddy
    - Bridget

Chart by John Goggins

234

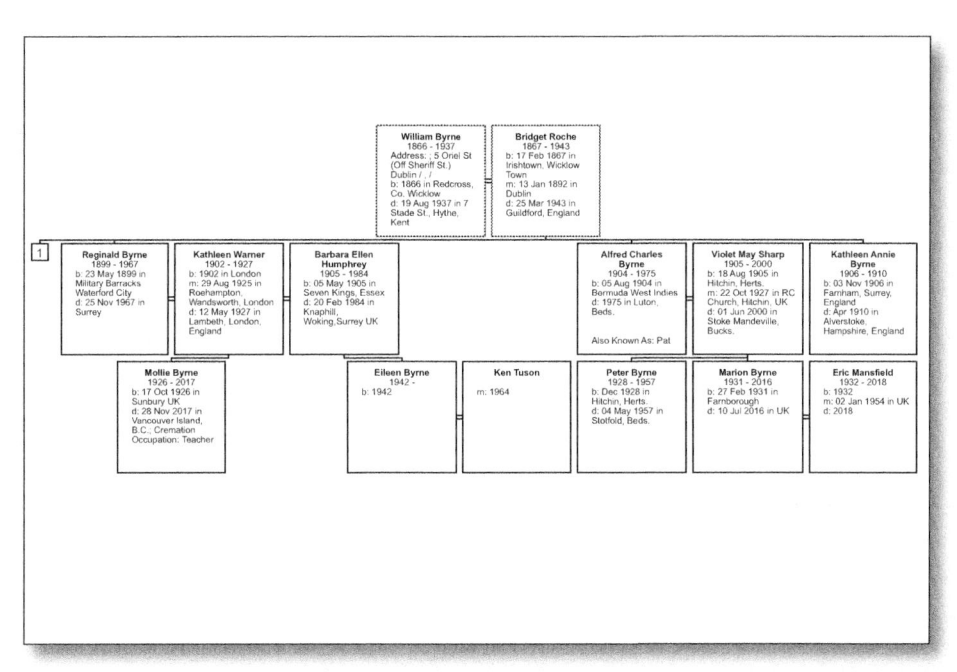

Chart 1

William Byrne 1866 - 1937
Address: ; 5 Oriel St (Off Sheriff St.) Dublin / , /
b: 1866 in Redcross, Co. Wicklow
d: 19 Aug 1937 in 7 Stade St., Hythe, Kent

Bridget Roche 1867 - 1943
b: 17 Feb 1867 in Irishtown, Wicklow Town
m: 13 Jan 1892 in Dublin
d: 25 Mar 1943 in Guildford, England

Children:

- **Reginald Byrne** 1899 - 1967
  b: 23 May 1899 in Military Barracks Waterford City
  d: 25 Nov 1967 in Surrey
- **Kathleen Warner** 1902 - 1927
  b: 1902 in London
  m: 29 Aug 1925 in Roehampton, Wandsworth, London
  d: 12 May 1927 in Lambeth, London, England
- **Barbara Ellen Humphrey** 1905 - 1984
  b: 05 May 1905 in Seven Kings, Essex
  d: 20 Feb 1984 in Knaphill, Woking,Surrey UK
- **Alfred Charles Byrne** 1904 - 1975
  b: 05 Aug 1904 in Bermuda West Indies
  d: 1975 in Luton, Beds.
  Also Known As: Pat
- **Violet May Sharp** 1905 - 2000
  b: 18 Aug 1905 in Hitchin, Herts.
  m: 22 Oct 1927 in RC Church, Hitchin, UK
  d: 01 Jun 2000 in Stoke Mandeville, Bucks.
- **Kathleen Annie Byrne** 1906 - 1910
  b: 03 Nov 1906 in Farnham, Surrey, England
  d: Apr 1910 in Alverstoke, Hampshire, England

Grandchildren:

- **Mollie Byrne** 1926 - 2017
  b: 17 Oct 1926 in Sunbury UK
  d: 28 Nov 2017 in Vancouver Island, B.C.; Cremation
  Occupation: Teacher
- **Eileen Byrne** 1942 -
  b: 1942
- **Ken Tuson**
  m: 1964
- **Peter Byrne** 1928 - 1957
  b: Dec 1928 in Hitchin, Herts.
  d: 04 May 1957 in Stotfold, Beds.
- **Marion Byrne** 1931 - 2016
  b: 27 Feb 1931 in Farnborough
  d: 10 Jul 2016 in UK
- **Eric Mansfield** 1932 - 2018
  b: 1932
  m: 02 Jan 1954 in UK
  d: 2018

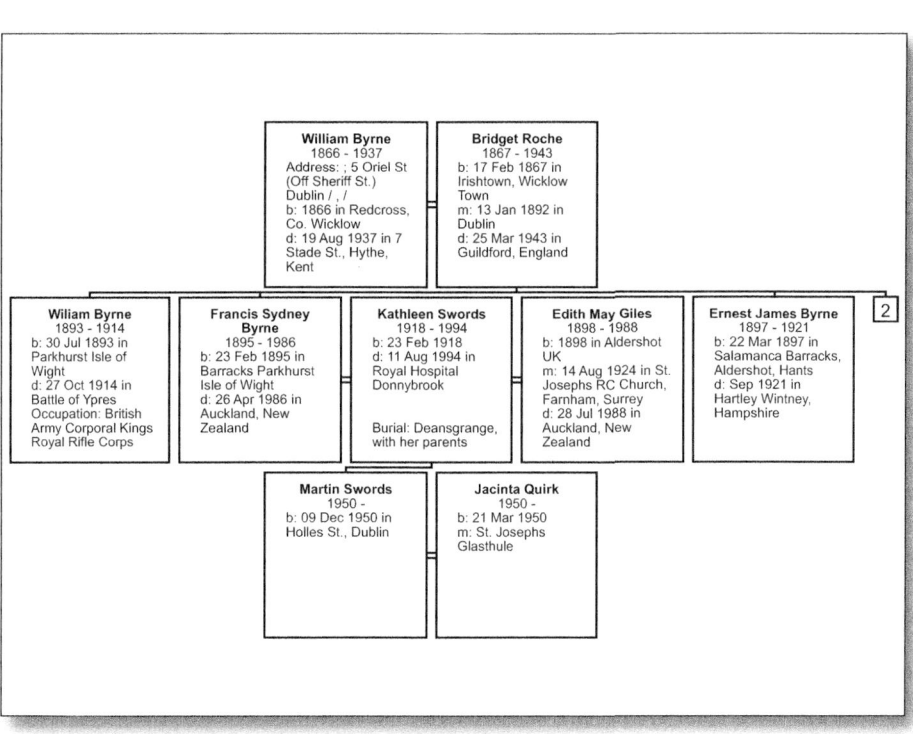

Chart 2

William Byrne 1866 - 1937
Address: ; 5 Oriel St (Off Sheriff St.) Dublin / , /
b: 1866 in Redcross, Co. Wicklow
d: 19 Aug 1937 in 7 Stade St., Hythe, Kent

Bridget Roche 1867 - 1943
b: 17 Feb 1867 in Irishtown, Wicklow Town
m: 13 Jan 1892 in Dublin
d: 25 Mar 1943 in Guildford, England

Children:

- **Wiliam Byrne** 1893 - 1914
  b: 30 Jul 1893 in Parkhurst Isle of Wight
  d: 27 Oct 1914 in Battle of Ypres
  Occupation: British Army Corporal Kings Royal Rifle Corps
- **Francis Sydney Byrne** 1895 - 1986
  b: 23 Feb 1895 in Barracks Parkhurst Isle of Wight
  d: 26 Apr 1986 in Auckland, New Zealand
- **Kathleen Swords** 1918 - 1994
  b: 23 Feb 1918
  d: 11 Aug 1994 in Royal Hospital Donnybrook
  Burial: Deansgrange, with her parents
- **Edith May Giles** 1898 - 1988
  b: 1898 in Aldershot UK
  m: 14 Aug 1924 in St. Josephs RC Church, Farnham, Surrey
  d: 28 Jul 1988 in Auckland, New Zealand
- **Ernest James Byrne** 1897 - 1921
  b: 22 Mar 1897 in Salamanca Barracks, Aldershot, Hants
  d: Sep 1921 in Hartley Wintney, Hampshire

Grandchildren:

- **Martin Swords** 1950 -
  b: 09 Dec 1950 in Holles St., Dublin
- **Jacinta Quirk** 1950 -
  b: 21 Mar 1950
  m: St. Josephs Glasthule

Regrets ? Just a Bit.

Regrets? Yes, I'd say there have been some regrets over the years. Regrets about what I knew, and when I knew it, and what my responses would have been if I had known things earlier. From that unforgettable 'Tea in the Burlington' conversation, through all the research online and within the wider family, through the struggles with St Patrick's Guild and Temple Hill, through the frustration of dealing with TUSLA and the office of the Information Commissioner, through the conversations with family relations who didn't really want to talk, through discovering Mollie Byrne in Canada, Francie Byrne in Auckland New Zealand, and my cousin Russ, and Judy, in England, much has been learned. But it has taken a lot of time. Tea in the Burlington was in 1987. Up to this point of writing this last chapter, still with a few bits yet to be found in 2021, 34 years have passed.

During all this time the regrets have varied, at times full of regrets for what I did not know. In later years the regrets have lessened with a more mature take on the story as a whole, to now when I might say I am almost glad I did not know more earlier.
Shortly after I learned the beginning of the story in The Burlington, I was full of angst, frustration, sadness, and

confusion. I wrote a series of poems and narratives which I put together into three short videos called 'Kathleen's Child', pts 1,2,3, It was subtitled 'things that should have been said', it was full of regret for all the things I should have said to Kathleen, to May and to Pat. It was all about the people and things I took for granted and the things I might have done for them by way of 'Thank You', but I was too busy being busy and getting ahead in life and career. Opportunities lost never come back.

In writing the 'Kathleen's Child' material I tried to imagine how the story looked from Kathleen's point of view, and from May's point of view. From Kathleen's point of view I'd like to think that this was a happy story. She had protected her baby. She had found or engineered a solution within the family that solved the dilemma and kept her close to her baby. She had prevented an adoption out of Temple Hill , I think it would have killed Kathleen if her baby had been adopted away, knowing the baby was out there somewhere, in America perhaps, and she not knowing where.

From May's point of view the story was both difficult and happy. Yes, she and Pat had a baby boy where they might not have had any children. But May adopted both the baby and the mother together so to speak, and this must have been difficult for her. I wonder if May had a fear over the years that at some point the baby would in some sense go back to Kathleen, physically or emotionally. I suspect that such a fear may have influenced May to move from the informal adoption, typical of the 1940s and 1950s, to the formal adoption after the introduction of adoption legislation in 1953. She may have been influenced in this decision to head off the possibility, by discussions with family, friends, or neighbours. In any case May, whose lack of education may have held her back from such complicated discussions on rights and wrongs, secured the adoption. Probably May held the fear all her life, that she would lose the baby's affection to Kathleen.

Pat had a more stoical attitude and just wanted everyone and everything to be happy. There was only so much he could do. I believe now that in 1950/51 when Kathleen had me and was looking for a solution, it was mostly down to Pat to agree that he and May would take the baby in. Whether he approached Kathleen with the proposed solution, quite possibly, or Kathleen approached Pat with the proposal, equally possible, I think it was largely Pat's decision and influence on May that resolved the matter. Though I acknowledge I might be a bit unfair towards May in this.

There had in those times been other babies born to unmarried mothers and adopted into family groups. Was this one so different ? Was this one so sensitive and so secret? Did this one have to be kept extra secret for a longer time ? I suspect this one was complicated by the close family connection with Francie being Kathleen's first cousin; she may not have known the term 'consanguinity' then, but she would have learnt it if she had sought permission from the local Parish Priest. Kathleen was asking no one.

A cousin of mine, Alice, whose mother Mary was the sister-in-law of May, told me that in a conversation with her mother once, her mother said that when I was around 16 Pat had said that he wanted to tell me I was adopted by him and May, and that Kathleen was my mother. But May did not want me to be told, so I wasn't. I have no reason to doubt the retelling, but it reinforces the belief that perhaps May was afraid of me being told.

Since 1987 and learning the beginning of this story, I have seen many internet comments from children and parents connected with Temple Hill, Saint Patrick's Guild, and the many Mother and Baby Homes throughout the country. I have heard too of the many 'Angels Plots' and burials in places like Tuam. There have been many horrific stories of neglect, abuse, forced adoption, and lifelong searches by mothers for children, and children for mothers. There have been many official reports and enquiries, books, documentaries, even films like 'Philomena'.

By comparison with such horrors, mine was a model story. My story had a fairytale dimension to it. I was greatly loved within a loving family. I had two Mammies. I had a great Daddy in Pat Swords. I had a biological father in Francis Sydney Byrne, and without disparaging him on little evidence, he went off early to look to his own needs. There was little we found to suggest he would have made a good Daddy. I had a great Natural Birth

Mother in Aunt Kathleen. A mother who fought tooth and nail for me. Lied on my Birth Certificate, kept visiting me and paying for my maintenance in the orphanage in Temple Hill. Went against the advice of the nuns and of her family and friends, and made sure I was not adopted. And she somehow engineered a solution within the family. She stayed close to me as I grew up and I've no doubt paid for my education and anything else required.

My wedding in 1974 must have been difficult for them all. Ma was there in her borrowed fur coat as the mother of the groom. Da was there in black tie suit, probably the first and only time in his life. Both proud as punch. Kathleen was there looking great, but not as the mother of the groom. It must have been difficult for both Kathleen and Ma. It was a great day, big party and lots to drink. I knew nothing at that time. I wonder how many people at the wedding knew about Kathleen's Child. Good job that with the drinking and dancing, no drunken uncle or aunt blurted out something they shouldn't have said. It does happen, more often than you might think.
So Kathleen, and Ma and Da said nothing all through my life. My life and theirs had settled down, and was fine, and no one was the worse for all keeping their secrets. When I thought about it a good while after I was told in the Burlington,
I realized that there was nothing to be gained and maybe a good deal to be lost, if I had been told earlier. I think Kathleen may have anticipated all of this. Martin was grown and married,

with two fine boys, David and Mark. And everyone in the family knew and loved Jacinta, his wife. All was good. Some or all of this could easily be put at risk if I had been told. Even without my meaning to, there could have been a subtle shift in the relationship between Ma and me, or between Kathleen and me. If there was a difference, and it was seen by Ma as changing things, it could have been very hurtful and upsetting for her. It could have upset the relationship between Ma and Kathleen. Probably best to leave well enough alone.

Did Kathleen want to tell me earlier in life? I dare say she did. Yet in not telling me earlier, she continued to protect me; to protect Ma, and to protect the chemistry and good relationships within the family. She was looking after everyone as ever.

I now think she was right not to say anything earlier. The whole family bond was not broken, so why say anything that might break it. The way she had played it so far had worked well, so why put it at risk.

Why then did she tell me when she did over Tea at the Burlington in 1987? Well I think the opportunity may just have fallen into her lap given the occasion, and the particular set of questions raised in the conversation. It may have been on her mind for a time and she seized the moment when she found it. She may also have been thinking that given her age and state of health, she should deal with this issue the way she wanted to. That's why I think she only told us as much as we needed and was able to emphasize the need to protect Ma in all of this by making Jacinta and I promise not to let Ma know that we knew. Pat Swords had died 9 years earlier in 1978, 18th January, aged 63, in Walters pub in Dún Laoghaire while having a pint, which was only half finished. He was dead and gone before I learned the story. I would have liked to have spoken to Pat about it, I'm sure I would have learned a lot.

Ma, Mary Swords, died suddenly in 1989, in my house actually, where she was babysitting David and Mark, while Jacinta and I were at Goffs in Kildare. I worked at the time for Gallahers, and I was in Goffs dealing with the company's sponsorship of the Benson and Hedges Irish Masters Snooker. The two boys, when Ma collapsed, had the good sense to go up the road to get Jacinta's dad, Sean Quirk, their Grandad, to come down to the house, but Ma was gone.

Kathleen herself died as I said earlier in Donnybrook Hospital on 11th August 1994.
I think if she had wanted to, she could have taken her story to the grave. Perhaps she realised that the story for me and my family would have been an even bigger shock to learn after she had passed on, and probably a bigger job to untangle and understand.

So regrets? Only a few. I understand the story better now even though it has been all over the place in the telling. It's not been a story easy to tell very smoothly, the dramatic news learned late meant that everything looked different looking back. I spent the second half of the story finding out about the first half of the story. It won't be shortlisted for the Booker Prize. But it's my story and it's told my way.

I have told parts of this story over the years and presented my video Kathleen's Child to many groups, family history groups, community and retirement groups. The story was received to hushed attention, as we say in Ireland, 'not a dry eye in the house'. It was striking for me on a few occasions at these presentations, that someone in the audience would say to me 'I knew your mother Kathleen, she was a lovely lady'.

She was indeed.

*Jacinta and I at a Debs Dance for St Joseph of Cluny,
held in the old Jury's on Dame Street.
We were 'Schoolgate' sweethearts, since before our Leaving Cert
in 1969, and yes, I did carry her schoolbooks home.
We got married in 1974.*

Informal photographs from the wedding.

An intriguing photograph and message.
Sent by Jock, a boyfriend, to Kathleen in October 1952.
As I had been taken out of Saint Patrick's Guild, Temple Hill in
October 1951, and placed informally with Pat and May in Booterstown,
we don't know where, when or how Kathleen and Jock met. This message is
dated October 1952, though the photo may have been taken earlier.
Looking at the picture and message they seem happy together.
But they did not stay together, this may have been a parting message.

Whispers in the family memories suggest that her mother Ellen was not happy about Jock taking Kathleen off to Scotland, indeed there may well have been a Catholic/Protestant issue. Kathleen may have wanted to stay to care for her mother Ellen, who died less than three years later. Kathleen may also have wanted to stay at home to be close to me, and to have access, and play a big part in my upbringing. This was probably an important consideration, and may always have been part of her long term plan, and so it transpired.

Notes and Letters

Date of Application	11.4.'51
Child's Name	Martin M. Burke
Date of Birth 9.12.50	Place of Birth Holles St.
Date of Baptism 13.12.50	Place of Baptism W. Row
Has child been registered?	Has child been vaccinated
Expectant Mother's name	Kathleen Evans (Mrs Burke)
Expectant Mother's occupation	Shop assist
Married or Single	
Baby expected	Born
First Pregnancy	Yes
Age 32	B.W.R. Test
Place of Origin	Dublin
Parish Dolphins	Diocese Dublin
Recommended by Mrs Joggins (Sister)	
Putative Father's name & address	Thos Burke, East Wall Road
Is Putative Father a relative of applicant?	No
Conditions of Payment (amount per week for maintenance of child)	£70 adoption
Responsible for Payment	c/o Mrs Joggins
Mother's present address	29 Long Av. Dolphins barn
Mother's parents' address	19 ... Dolphins barn
In case of illness how is applicant to be notified?	
When was applicant last at the Sacraments?	

REMARKS: Father dead, Mother alive & aware
adm to T.H. 17.4.'51

IMPORTANT.
BABY'S BIRTH AND BAPTISMAL CERTIFICATES ESSENTIAL WHEN CHILD IS TAKEN.

The Application

THIS AGREEMENT made between St.Patrick's Guild (hereinafter called The Guild) of 50,Middle Abbey Street,Dublin, of the one part and *Kathleen Burke* . OF THE other part and dated as hereunder jointly and severally for ourselves our executors and administrators agree to pay the Honoray Secretary or Honorary Treasurer of the said Guild for the time being the sum of £ *2* monthly for the maintenance of the child *Martin Mary Burke* while *he* remains in the custody of St.Patrick's Guild such payments to start from the *17th* day of *April* 194*8.51* and we hereby expressly understand and agree with the Guild that "IT" (The Guild) should only be responsible for the care custody and maintenance of the said child as the aforesaid payments are punctually made by us and we further agree with the Guild that should any default be made by us in the payments all responsibility for the care custody and maintenance by or on behalf of the Guild to absolutely cease and determine as from ten days after date of last payment made by us and that under this Agreement we thereupon shall take over the responsibility as theretofore undertaken by the Guild. I further agree to remove the child from the custody of St.Patrick's Guild should I fail to keep mt Agreement.

SIGNED *Kathleen Burke* WITNESS *(Mr) G. Groggins*

SIGNED *Kathleen Burke* WITNESS *(Mrs) G. Groggins*

The Signed Agreement

*My Baptism as Martin Mary Burke 13th December 1950.
I have never been baptised in my real name.*

St. Patrick's Guild, Dublin. (Founded 1910)

INCORPORATED

Under the care of The Irish Sisters of Charity
WITH THE APPROVAL OF HIS GRACE THE ARCHBISHOP OF DUBLIN

PHONE 74531
After Office Hours 81238
Office Hours, 1 to 12 30 p.m.
                1 3 to 3 p.m
Saturdays 10 a.m. to 1 p.m.

PLEASE QUOTE
REF No

All Communications to be addressed to
SISTER IN CHARGE,
50 MIDDLE ABBEY STREET
DUBLIN

CERTIFICATE OF SURRENDER.

I hereby certify that I have this _14th_ day of _April_ 19_51_ handed over my child _Martin Mary_ to the custody of St. PATRICK'S GUILD, 50, Middle Abbey Street, Dublin. I surrender _him_ completely and entirely. I solemnly promise that I shall not interfere with _him_ in any way whatsoever in the future.

SIGNED _Kathleen Burke_
WITNESSED _Sr. F. Elizabeth_
DATE _14. 4. 51_

Certificate of Surrender

St. Patrick's Guild, Dublin.

(INCORPORATED)

FOUNDED 1910

Telephone
(01) 668 1765
(01) 668 1908

Office Hours:
Mon to Fri.
10 to 5 p.m.

REGISTERED ADOPTION SOCIETY

UNDER THE CARE OF THE IRISH SISTERS OF CHARITY
WITH THE APPROVAL OF HIS GRACE THE ARCHBISHOP OF DUBLIN

82 HADDINGTON ROAD,
DUBLIN 4.

21st January 1998.

Private & Confidential

Mr. Martin Swords,
5 Knocknacree Road,
Dalkey,
Co. Dublin.

Dear Mr. Swords,

I received your letter of enquiry in January. Thank you for your generous donation of £25 to St. Patrick's Guild. Sr. Gabriel Murphy retired at the end of last February and I took her from her in March.

We will be glad to help you in anyway that we can with your enquiry. I have checked and located your record here. Your letter of February 5th, 1996 is on the record. It seems to have been filed before a reply was sent to you. I regret this very long delay in responding to your request.

Our record shows that you were born on December 9th 1950 at the National Maternity Hospital, Holles Street and baptised at St. Andrew's Church, Westland Row on December 13th, 1950. On both your birth and baptismal certificates you were registered as Martin Mary Burke, the son of Thomas and Kathleen (nee Swords) Burke. The sponsors at your baptism were James and Anne Goggins. From the copy of the birth certificate which you enclosed it is clear that your mother Kathleen Swords corrected the entry in the Birth Register on April 5th, 1954 by means of a statutory declaration.

You were admitted to St. Patrick's, Temple Hill, on April 17th, 1951 and discharged to your mother on October 30, 1951. St. Patrick's provided nursery care during that period. You might like to know that on November 23rd, 1951 Kathleen wrote to Sr. Francis Elizabeth to

> "... let you know how Baby Burke has been going on. He settled into his new home at once and is quite happy there. They are all delighted with him ..."

She goes on to ask that your ration book be sent on and this was done on November 29, 1951. There was no further correspondence.

St. Patrick's Guild - 21 January 1998

If there is anything in the above information that you wish to discuss further please contact me and an appointment can be arranged.

Wishing you every happiness and blessing during this New Year.

Yours sincerely,

Sister Francis Ignatius Fahy,
Director.

St. Patrick's Guild, Dublin

(INCORPORATED)
REGISTERED ADOPTION SOCIETY
UNDER THE CARE OF THE RELIGIOUS SISTERS OF CHARITY

27th March, 1998.

Mr. Martin Swords,
5 Knocknacree Road,
Dalkey,
Co. Dublin.

Dear Mr. Swords,

Following our meeting at the end of January I made copies of the letters from Mrs. Annie Goggins but unfortunately I got no further than that. My apologies for this delay.

As you were able to fill in the fact that Annie was not long married herself at that time the concern, distress and anxiety which she expressed are both understandable and appropriate in the circumstances. It was a very difficult situation for her. Nevertheless, your mother Kathleen was determined that she was not going to lose sight of you. She maintained her contributions towards your upkeep and maintenance on a regular basis until you were placed in her care on October 30th, 1951. On July 19 she had cancelled the certificate of surrender which she had signed earlier on April 14, 1951.

I am enclosing a copy of your original baptismal certificate and as you will see Jim and Annie Goggins were your sponsors.

You already have a copy of your original birth certificate. I notice that Kathleen amended the original registration by Statutory Declaration on April 5th, 1954. The certificate from the Adopted Children's Register states that the Adoption Order in your regard was made on November 22, 1954. This would seem to indicate that your mother Kathleen amended the original certificate in order to allow Patrick and Mary Swords to adopted you legally. With the introduction of legal adoption in 1953 this option would have been open to them but only if the original registration of the birth was amended to show that you were not the son of a married couple. I cannot recall if we spoke of this when you were here but as I have been working recently on a situation where an adoption order could not be made because of the original certificate, and so it is fresh in my mind just now. The fact that you obtained a copy of your certificate form

82, Haddington Road, Dublin 4   Tel: (01) 668 1765 (01) 668 1908 Fax: (01) 668 6234

St. Patrick's Guild - 27 March 1998

the Adopted Children's Register and that there is a date for the adoption order (Nov. 22, 1954) confirms that you were legally adopted by Patrick and Mary Swords.

I am now checking with Holles Street to see if there is any more information available there. I will also contact the Adoption Board to see if they have anything. However, as St. Patrick's Guild did not make the arrangements for the adoption it is possible that they may not release any information to us.

There is just one other letter that may have a bearing on your situation. It was written by a Kate Forde on April 6th, 1952 from a Cork hospital. She writes of how pleased she is that all is going well for 'little Martin'. She refers to the fact that she brought him to the Guild. But it would appear from Anne Goggins' letter that she (Anne) came with Kathleen to bring you in. However perhaps you can make some discreet enquiries yourself as to whether or not there was a relative or friend of that name who worked in Cork.

As soon as I hear from the Adoption Board or from Holles Street I will let you know.

With every good wish.

Sr. Francis Ignatius Fahy
Sister Francis Ignatius Fahy,
Director.

Copies enclosed of:
Letter from Annie Goggins April 14, 1951 and July 27, 1951.
Agreement signed by Kathleen and Annie April 17, 1951.
'Certificate of Surrender' April 14, 1951. Cancelled July 19, 1951.
Original Baptismal Certificate
Letter from St. Patrick's Guild to Mrs. Annie Goggins July 30, 1951.

This letter was received on April 14, 1951.

4501

27 Corrig Avenue,
Dun Laoghaire
Co. Dublin.

Dear Sr. Frances Elizabeth,

This is Mrs. Goggins again, I tried to phone you several times yesterday and to day but did not get any reply. I wanted to let you know with regard to the form Kathleen got to fill up, that I will pay the ten shillings weekly until she has a little time to look after her health and get herself a job. I wonder if it will do to fill in that form in your office, when we get word to bring in the child, as I could not put in the date now, as I presume the payments will only begin when a home has been found for the baby.

Kathleen is going to Holles St in the morning about the blood test. We can do no more now but hope and pray that you will be able to take the baby as quickly as possible. Please Sr. Frances hurry things up if you can, things are really desperate with us and it is quite impossible for my husband and myself to keep the girl any longer

Letter to Sr. Francis Elizabeth from Mrs. Annie Goggins
14 April 1951

relations are very strained in my home and I am torn between my duty to my husband and affection for my family and my anxiety to help them out. We have managed to keep this secret so far and if it were to come out now it would cause a great scandal and the girl would not get a day's work in the place, as well as disgracing the rest of the family who are trying to earn their living in the town, and I will surely lose my home if something is not done quickly to help.

When Kathleen is working there will be no fear of defaulting in the payments as she is most anxious that the child should have a good catholic home. I know her life will be one of remorse and regret as we were a very happy and united family until this one slip of hers, and we will never be the same again, but there is no use in telling her to start life anew if she does not get some practical help now. She cannot look after soul or body until the baby gets a home. I have not the heart to condemn her, as any one of us could say, but for the grace of God, there go I. Hoping to hear from you soon,

I remain,
Yours Respectfully,
(Mrs) Annie Goggins.

*Acknowledge — would
I letter will have
will have a little with
the girl —*

30 JUL

29 Boring Avenue.
Dun Laoghaire.
27/7/51

Dr Sr Frances E Elizabeth,

This is Mrs Goggins to worry you again about my sister Kathleen. Since she has been seeing the baby at the home each month, she has done nothing but weep and fret from one visit to another, and I know now it was not a good idea to urge that she be allowed to see him at all, but we hoped he would have been adopted long ago.

She is full of the idea that she can take the baby out of the home again, but she has nowhere to take it to. She cannot take it to her old and feeble mother, and she must work herself to earn her living. My husband and I have given her all the help we can over this affair, you know how hard I pleaded to get a home for the child and how we thanked God believing we were doing the right thing for the girl in helping her to start her life anew and put the past behind

Letter to Sr. Francis Elizabeth from Mrs. Annie Goggins
27 July 1951

her, but it seems now as if it were all to be in vain. We thought the whole affair was finished and done with for ever, and we never intended to bring up the subject again even with our own family but let it be forgotten. Kathleen had resumed her normal life, living with her mother and going to work each day and should have been happy and contented, instead of making herself and everyone else miserable.

   I am sure you will agree that after all the trouble and sorrow the family have suffered on her account it would be a very grave thing to rake up all that scandal in the district now after having kept it a secret so long. She has some rash plan about a cousin looking after the child, but that cousin only lives in a small house in the next street to us, and has four children of her own, so that would be like bringing it home. I know Sr Frances that you will think well over all this, I felt I must write to you as I have taken on myself to be in a way responsible for her, but she is not to be told that I have written to you. She would

30 JUL 1951

never forgive me. I hope you will try to have the child adopted as soon as possible and in the meantime we think it adviseable that she does not see the baby again. I am sure you will advise her, when next she visits you that this is the only course open to her and will be all for the best.

   I Remain,
   Yours Sincerely,
 (Mrs)   Annie Goggins.

SCE   30th. July, '51.

Mrs. Annie Goggins,
29 Corrig Avenue,
<u>Dun Laoghaire.</u>

Dear Mrs. Goggins,

        Many thanks for yours received this morning. I am sorry to see by it that you are so worried, but please God everything will work out right in the end. We will have a little talk with Kathleen. Do not be worrying. God has protected you up to this and He will watch over you in the future too. Pray for Kathleen. It is only natural that she would get fond of the child but with God's grace she will act wisely concerning it.

        Wishing you every grace and blessing.

        Yours sincerely in J.C.

        Sister-in-Charge.

Reply from Sister-in-Charge - 30 July 1951

St. Patrick's Guild, Dublin

(INCORPORATED)
REGISTERED ADOPTION SOCIETY
UNDER THE CARE OF THE RELIGIOUS SISTERS OF CHARITY

11th August 1998.

Mr. Martin Swords
5, Knocknacree Road,
Dalkey
Co. Dublin.

Dear Martin,

Thank you for your letter "reminder" received to-day.

I did check with Holles Street, and received a few more details. Unfortunately I filed the letter and omitted to write to you. My apologies for this oversight and consequent long delay in sending you the information.

There is no medical chart for 1950. The details that are available are that

"Mrs. Kathleen Burke was admitted to this hospital on the 9th December, 1950 and she gave birth to a healthy male infant at 9.20pm, normal delivery. Her age at the time of delivery is noted to be 32years, her husband's name is given as Thomas and his occupation is given as factory labourer. The address is a little unclear on the entry, but it looks like 29(or24) Corrig Avenue, Dun Laoghaire. There is no details of birth weight on the record and it appears to have been a first pregnancy. No further information is available.

I have written to the Adoption Board also and have requested that they send any information either directly to your or back to me for you. As the adoption was not arranged through St. Patrick's Guild the Board may not wish to release the information to us.

With every good wish.

Yours sincerely,

Sister Francis Ignatius Fahy,
Director.

82, Haddington Road, Dublin 4. Tel: (01) 668 1765 (01) 668 1908 Fax: (01) 668 6234

St. Patrick's Guild - 11 August 1998

St. Patrick's Guild, Dublin

(INCORPORATED)
REGISTERED ADOPTION SOCIETY
UNDER THE CARE OF THE RELIGIOUS SISTERS OF CHARITY

Mr. Martin Swords
5, Knocknacree Road,
Dalkey
Co. Dublin.   23. September 1998.

Dear Martin,

Thank you for your letter of September 17th last.

The information which you have obtained is of the kind that only family members know. It is quite amazing how much information is retained within the wider family circle- if one puts the questions to the "right" person! I am very pleased for you that you have been able to build up a more complete picture of your own family background. Your search has been a diligent one. *Thank you for telling me about it all!*

There is no reference whatsoever to Francis Byrne here. The only name we have for your father is that of Thomas Burke. This is the name that was given on both your original birth and baptismal certificates. As you know this name was later removed from the birth certificate by your mother Kathleen Swords.

I did make an inquiry to the Adoption Board and received a reply on September 17th when I returned to the office. There is no additional information available from the record held there.

It does seem that St. Patrick's Guild can not offer any further help to you in your search. Perhaps within the extended family there will be some record of Francis Byrne's address or the area in which he lived in New Zealand. It is not such not such a vast country. This may enable you to contact other family members, perhaps other sons and daughters of Francis! Given his age in 1950 it is highly unlikely that he is still living himself. It remains for me simply to wish you every success if you do decide to continue with your efforts.

With every good wish,

Yours sincerely,

Francis Ignatius Fahy
Sister Francis Ignatius Fahy.

82, Haddington Road, Dublin 4. Tel: (01) 668 1765 (01) 668 1908 Fax: (01) 668 6234

St. Patrick's Guild - 23 September 1998

16 December 1999

Mr. Martin Swords
97 Ballinclea Heights
Killiney
Co. Dublin.

Dear Martin,

It was good to hear from you recently. Thank you for your generous donation of £25.00, your thoughtfulness is much appreciated.

What you say about your birth mother's friend Marina and the information she was able to give you was quite remarkable. It was also good to have the name Francis Byrne confirmed. There are no other details or papers here that would add to your story. Indeed you have rounded out your story very well and mostly by your own diligent search.

It remains for me to wish you every blessing and happiness this Christmastide and in the Jubilee Year.

Yours sincerely,

Sr. Francis
Sr. Francis I. Fahy,
Director.

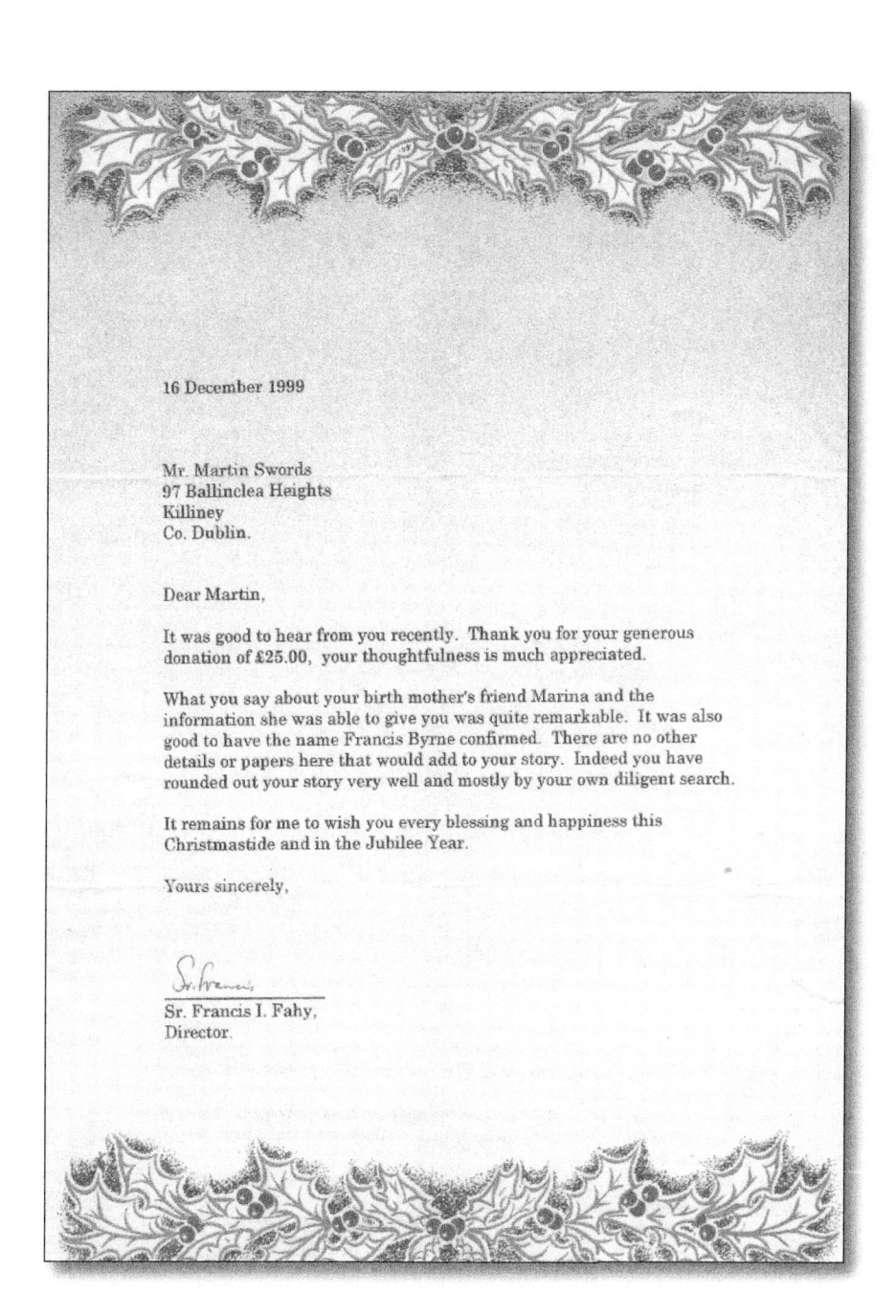

Christmas Letter - 1999

DESPERATELY SEEKING FRANCIE BYRNE

(Francis Sydney Byrne)

Information sought, address, family, descendents, photos, etc.

Francie Byrne, family late of Wicklow, Ireland and Woking, Surrey, England. Moved New Zealand early 1950's, married to a schoolteacher (?). Businessman, Investor, some connection with Irish Sweepstakes. Possibly deceased at this stage.

Details sought re legacy in Ireland.

Written replies to:
**Legal Secretary,
M.S.A. Management,
76 Upper Georges Street,
Dun Laoghaire,
Co. Dublin, Ireland.
Fax: 01-2301122**

A shot in the dark,
press advertisement placed in New Zealand Press.
Did not work.

19 Findlater St.
Sandycove.
23-11-51

24 NOV 1951

Dear Sister Francis Elizabeth
 I had intended going in to see you one day to let you know how Baby Burke has been going on. He settled in to his new home at once and is quite happy there. They are all delighted with him but I have been asked time and time again for his ration book so if you could send them on to me I would be very pleased as it is time to lodge new pages now. I will drop in and see you one day. Thanking you very much for all you have done for me.
 I remain
  Yours faithfully
  K. Swords.

Letter to Sr. Francis Elizabeth - 24 November 1951

SCB

29th. Nov. '51.

Miss K. Swords,
19, Findlater Street,
Sandycove,
DUBLIN.

Dear Miss Swords,

      Many thanks for your nice letter. I am very glad to know little Baby Burke is so well and so settled down. I am sending you his Ration Book and I regret delay in sending it on to you.

      With every kind wish and may God bless you.

      Yours sincerely in J.C.

Reply from Sister-in-Charge - 29 November 1951

1563 Sherwood Dr.
Nanaimo, B.C.
V9T 1H1
Feb 14

Dear Martin,

It was very interesting to hear from you and I am very puzzled to know how you learned about me from the "Estuary Book"!? This was just a work book that I wrote for my grade 11 Biology classes here in Nanaimo. I had a grant from the University of British Columbia in Vancouver, where I went to do the work. It was never published, just copies made for my gr. 11 classes. Was it the Internet? By the way my e-mail address needs a small r.

mollyr@shaw.ca

I can pick up e-mails but there is a problem about sending them at the moment,

Letter to Martin from Mollie - 14 February 2012

but that should be solved quite soon.

Of course I knew both Kathleen Swords because my father (Reginald Byrne) took me to Ireland several times after the war, & her sister Ina came to live with my grand parents (Bridget & William) in Hythe, Kent, but she didn't stay very long. My uncle Francie was always known as a "ladies man" & guess that's true!! His wife was very strange & wouldn't let him invite anyone to the house. They emigrated to New Zealand, but I'm not sure of the date. I never knew about Kathleen giving birth to you – but you seem to have done alright with good wife & kids.

My next birthday is 85

& at the moment I have an injured foot, so it d seem too likely that I make it to Ireland — but never know.

I've been looking an up to date photo of & don't seem to have one, I'll keep looking the rolls of photos & will se later. Instead I'sending view from my kitchen w of whats called Departure with the ferries to Vanco in the background. The be I ever did for myself was come to Canada; a great in every sense of the word

So I'll end here & write again later.

All the best, & 1 for writing to me.

from

Mollie

⑦ 1563 Sherwood Dr
Nanaimo, BC
V9T 1H1
March 12

Dear Martin,

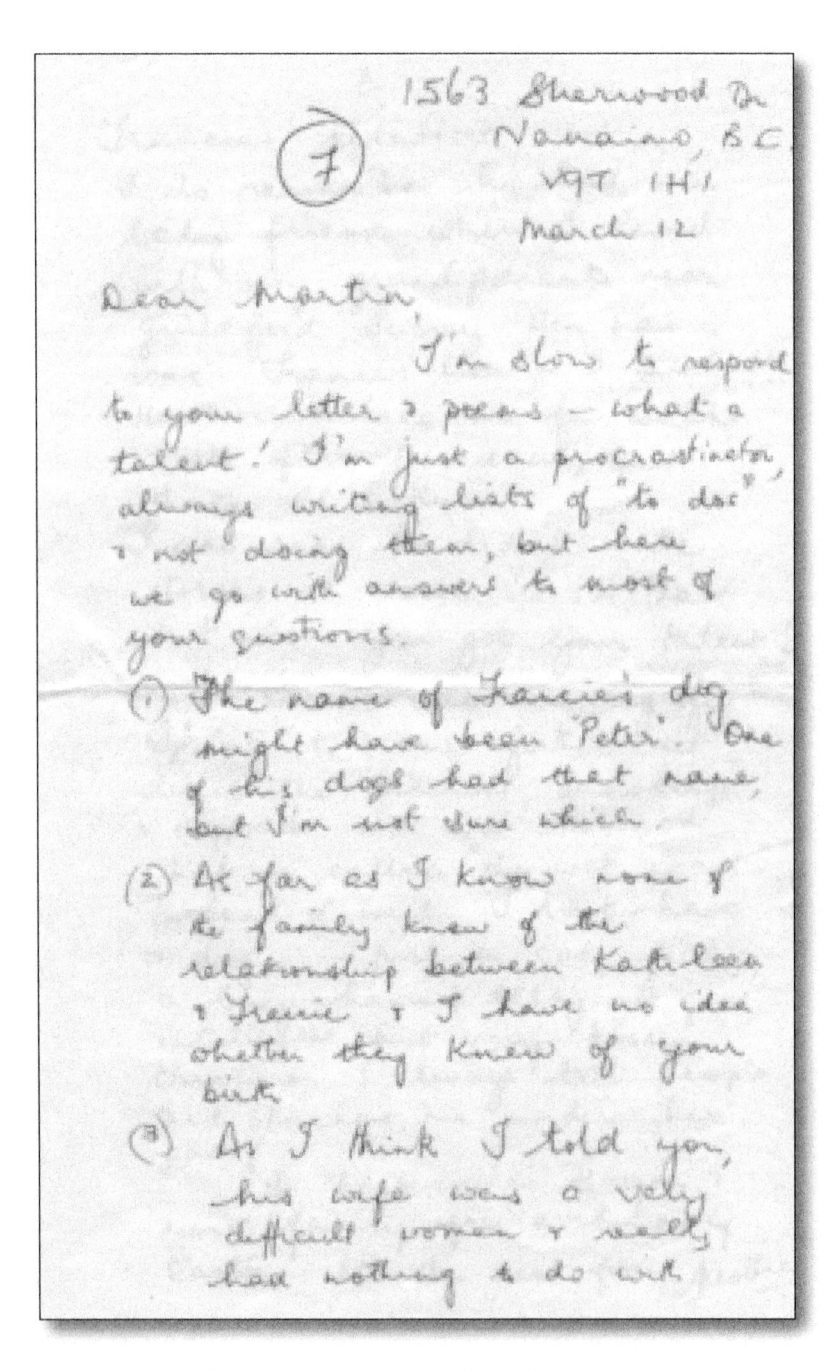

I'm slow to respond to your letter & poems — what a talent! I'm just a procrastinator, always writing lists of "to do" & not doing them, but here we go with answers to most of your questions.

(1) The name of Francie's dog might have been "Peter". One of his dogs had that name, but I'm not sure which.

(2) As far as I know none of the family knew of the relationship between Kathleen & Francie & I have no idea whether they knew of your birth.

(3) As I think I told you, his wife was a very difficult woman & really had nothing to do with

Letter to Martin from Mollie - 12 March

2

Frances' relatives.

I do remember he had one lady friend when I lived with my grandparents near Guildford, Surrey. Her name was Frances Lee - I think!! He would take me for walks & she often joined us, but that's all I know.

I am sure he didn't write stories or verse ..... that's not where you got your talent!

So we are waiting for Spring to come forth - at least the crocuses, snowdrops & daffodils are out, here on what is called "the wet coast" instead of west. I don't have a dog .... just a cat, Nicky, a long-haired tabby. A good, intelligent but very bossy creature. I always tell people that she has me under her paw!

So best wishes to you & your family for a happy Easter. All the best from prollie

1563 Sherwood Dr.
Nanaimo, B.C.
V9T 1H1
July 12

Dear Martin,
I'm so sorry that you won't have had a reply to your letter, book & poem. The problem is that we have had a postal strike, which delayed its arrival. The mail is now moving again so I can respond, belatedly!!

I haven't heard from Caroline Butler (Murphy) but will keep hoping. As I think I told you in my last letter, Sara came to live with my grandparents for a short time, at Hythe, in Kent.

My e-mail address is:

mollyr@shaw.ca. I am having trouble with sending — partly the computer & partly me, but one day soon I hope we (me & computer) will do better. Receiving e mails is no problem.

Letter to Martin from Mollie - 12 July ????

274

(Sorry about the marks on the paper —
I'm a dedicated recycler!)
Thank you very much for the
Larkin book & your poem. I
write little verses, so will send
some — mostly about cats!!
You didn't tell me how you
came across my Estuary book, &
I'm puzzled.
I loved the photo of St Kevin's
church — I love Glendalough.

No real news from this end —
we are having a very sub-standard
summer & so I've decided I must
take advantage of the stay home
weather to de-junk my house.
Well, I've done a little bit.

Thank you for thinking
of me & I'm sorry about the
delay.

All the best,
from
Mollie

1563 Sherwood Dr
Nanaimo
BC.
V9T 1H1
Nov 21/10

Dear John,

What wonderful research you have done! I'm proud of you. Francis Byrne's escapades do not surprise me; he was definitely a "ladies man" & his wife was quite strange — he couldn't even ask me into his home. I'm just going to dig out some old photos & see what I can match to your information.

I have been very slow to respond to your birthday greetings because I have been out of action following a stupid accident. I had gone up the street to feed a friend's cats & the sole

Letter to John from Mollie - 21 October 2010

of my shoe stuck to the stair carpet. I lost my balance & fell backwards onto the hardwood floor. An X-ray revealed nothing, but I eventually had a CT scan that revealed a fractured sacrum at base of the backbone & one damaged lumbar vertebra. I spent over 3 weeks in bed, looked after by kind friends and neighbours. There is nothing to be done except to let the bones heal themselves. Now I am hobbling around & have managed to drive out & go shopping, but not today as we are having our first snow. We don't get much here on the West Coast, but the ski hills are pleased to be able to open early.

I hear on the news that Ireland is having a bad financial time, so hope it doesn't affect you. Canada is fortunate to be in better shape than most countries.

So I send Christmas greetings and ask you to pass on my wishes to any of the "clan" who remember us. Happy Christmas to you both.

from,

Mollie

1563 Sherwood Dr
Nanaimo BC
V9T 1H1
Nov 25 '12

Dear Martin,
At last I have got around to digging out some old photographs & am sending some on to you. How photography has changed! There is a little information about Kenore on them. I think I told you that his wife (Edith??) was strange & wouldn't let anyone drop in, let alone visit.

As I am now nearer 90 than 80 (86!) I am trying to de-junk my house — I can't believe how much paper stuff I have accumulated. So I think you had better think of this as your

Letter to Martin from Mollie - 25 November 2012

Christmas card — haven't started on those yet & I have a long list. Your climate is very like ours on Vancouver Island so I expect you'll have a green christmas. Enjoy!

All best wishes,
Mollie

St. Patrick's Guild, Dublin. (Founded 1910)

INCORPORATED

Under the care of The Irish Sisters of Charity

WITH THE APPROVAL OF HIS GRACE THE ARCHBISHOP OF DUBLIN

PHONE 74531
After Office Hours 82258
Office Hours. 10 to 12.30 p.m.
2.15 to 5 p.m.
Saturdays. 10 a.m. to 1 p.m.

PLEASE QUOTE
REF. NO.............

All Communications to be addressed to
SISTER IN CHARGE,
50 MIDDLE ABBEY STREET
DUBLIN

Cancelled per telephone 19.7.51

CERTIFICATE OF SURRENDER.

I hereby certify that I have this 14th day of April 1951 handed over my child Martin Mary to the custody of St. PATRICK'S GUILD, 50, Middle Abbey Street, Dublin. I surrender him completely and entirely. I solemnly promise that I shall not interfere with him in any way whatsoever in the future.

SIGNED _Kathleen Swords._
WITNESSED _Sr. J. Elizabeth_
DATE _14.4.51_

Certificate of Surrender - Cancelled

P.O.Box 10030
Balmoral, Auckland
New Zealand.
May 15th.1965

Dear Mollie,
        It was such a shock to get a letter from you that it has taken me quite a long time to get over it. I did expect to get a Christmas Card from you but gave you up when it did not materialise, it was nice to hear from you and to hear that you are enjoying life in Vancouver. I did hear that the Woking folks were contemplating a trip to see you and I was going to suggest that they make the round trip and call to N.Z. as it is almost as cheap to do round the owrld as it is to go to B.C. & back, Pa has always wanted to see Bermuda so they could take that in also.
I am in trouble with my Mercedes cars but I actually have one (No 2) here and I am using it daily, it is really to good for what I want but I cannot dispose of it and actually I only have it here on a tourist licence for 12 months, after that Id dont know unless the owner comes out. The number one is at present in Sydney Australia I am going over there soon and will use it there for a time and eventually bring it to N.Z. They have closed down on the car racket here and there have been lots of court cases and lots of cars confiscated thro illegal entry but they have not put the finger on me yet and I have 2 Mercedes Benz cars two houses and no money.
I have just sold my house here £6,250, I gave £4,500 for it five years ago, value has gone up as it had nearly ½ acre and I obtained a permit to build 5 flats in addition to the house. I have bought another house £4,650, a nice place, English type, brick and nice looking with possibilities, I dont expect to be in it too long as we are contemplating a trip to U.K. and may even stay there. N.Z. has got very expensive everything goes up and up and we poor old age pensioners feel the pinch a bit, over 70 now, poor old fella as they would say in Dublin. I am swimming most days and the weather here is quite good yet this would be the same as mid November in England, there are not many swimmers about and sometimes I have the sea to myself Edie says just showing off but I go in mostly when there are no people there at all, there are some very nice beaches here and it is quite an interesting country so you had better make a trip sometime while we are here, we have pots of room and you can have a car with chauffer if you wish. If the folks come out I can lend them a house for a month, Reg does not like the heat but Im sure he likes the winter less. Lots of people here including myself have got the wind up about the future, it is predicted that the Chinese and Indonesians will be knocking at the door soon, I'll bet that it happens in your lifetime, N.Z. and Australia will be lost

Letter from Francie to Mollie, May 1965
Schemes and Plots and Plans

to the asiatics, the writing is on the wall, I think that you will
be safe in Vancouver unless from the earthquakes which appear to be
in your district, we have them here regularly and I have felt two
tremors, quite a weird experience, it is predicted that we are due
for a major earthquake.
We had a special football match here yesterday, they play mostly
rugby here but with so many immigrants coming soccer is getting its
share of support, the two football teams were Sheffield United and
Blackpool, they played each other as there are no teams good enough
for them here.
The lottery business has flopped here now as N.Z. has its own which
are very popular, a 5/- to win £12,000 (drawn every five days) and
a £1 to win £60,000 drawn six time a year so Irelands effort is very
poor these days and I do not look for business much. When I come to
Canada again I am going to try to put over the N.S.W. Opera House
£3 to win £100,000 run from Sydney every 14 days. this should go
well in Canada and U.S.A. so I am going to try it. I may send you
an envelope with some forms of application, just keep them until I
come.
I can immagineEileen and her condition, I bet she is kicking up a
a row, she is a bit of a madam and wanted a good spanking occasionally
as she was very disagreeable and unpleasant to her Ma and Pa sometimes
I did not like her much and sending her to a university was just a
waste of time and money. I hope you are still single, its best that
way.
I want you to send me a Vancouver paper, they usually have aspecial
day for advertising houses for sale and to let thats the one I want,
we might even come and stay for a few months if we can get a flat
and from what I saw in Vancouver it is easier than it is here.
If I come by myself I will bring a Caravan made up on a Bedford Chassis
they sell in England for £1000 and are just what I want for travelling
as I like to have my own place rather than hotels.
I have not heard from Woking lately but perhaps it is my turn to
write, I'll do so soon and suggest that round trip.
When we move out of this house we will miss all the fruit, tons of
grapefruit are just turning colour, pears, apples nectarines oranges
and guavas which you possibly dont know.
Thats all dear Edie sends her regards and would like to see you in
Vancouver sometime.

    Love from

    Francis

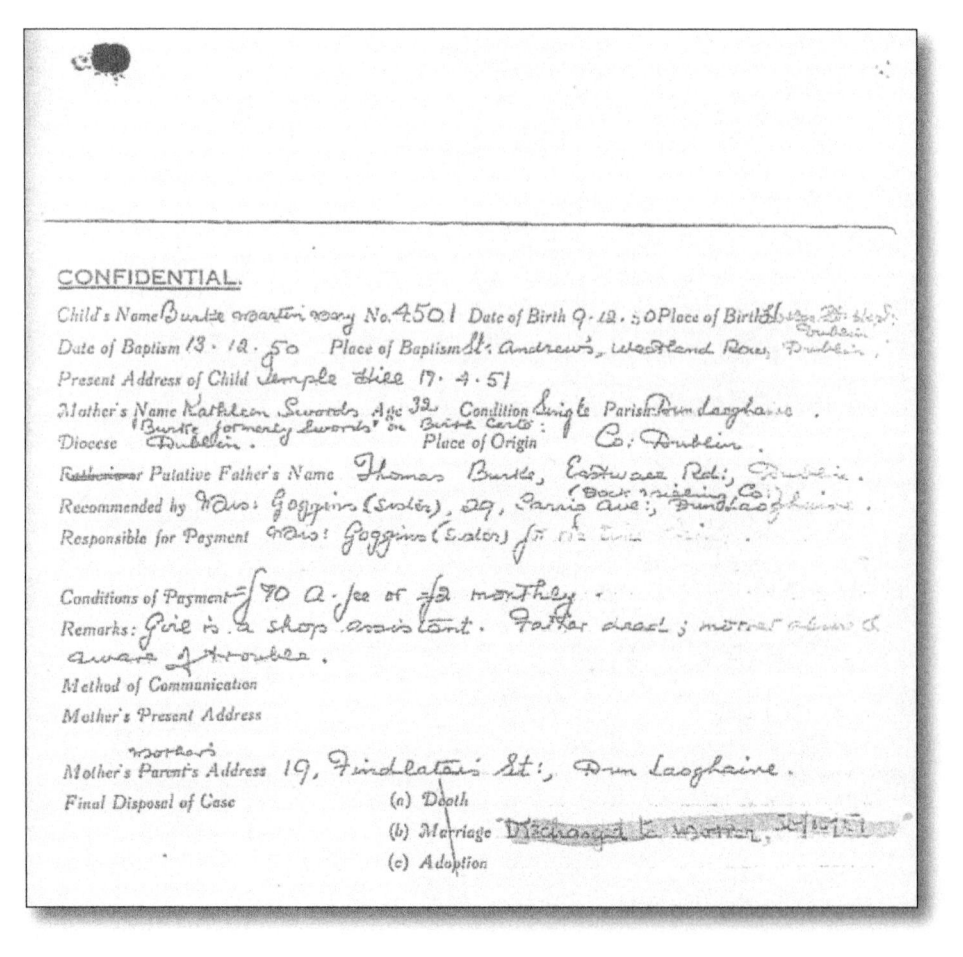

CONFIDENTIAL.

Child's Name Burke Martin Mary No. 4501 Date of Birth 9.12.50 Place of Birth Dublin
Date of Baptism 13.12.50 Place of Baptism St. Andrew's, Westland Row, Dublin
Present Address of Child Temple Hill 17.4.51
Mother's Name Kathleen Swords Age 32 Condition Single Parish Dun Laoghaire.
Diocese Dublin. 'Burke formerly Swords' on Birth Cert. Place of Origin Co. Dublin.
Putative Father's Name Thomas Burke, Eastwase Rd., Dublin. (Dock working Co.)
Recommended by Miss Goggins (Sister), 29, Carrig Ave., Dunlaoghaire.
Responsible for Payment Miss Goggins (Sister) —

Conditions of Payment £70 a. fee of £2 monthly.
Remarks: Girl is a shop assistant. Father dead; mother alone & aware of trouble.
Method of Communication
Mother's Present Address
Mother's Parent's Address 19, Findlater's St., Dun Laoghaire.
Final Disposal of Case
(a) Death
(b) Marriage Discharged to mother, 24/12/51
(c) Adoption

Confidential

Poems arising from this story

All a Wonder

At seven, all a wonder.
The boy with his Aunt Kathleen
snug in bed, stone hot water
bottle in its blanket, keeping
October frost outside.

Streetlight shines through net curtains
casting paisley patterns on the wall.
Moving. Changing with the breeze,
their own picture show.

Talking about the big wide world.
Tales of the Galapagos.
Exploring Easter Island
and the Pyramids.
He knew the Orinoco and the Nile.
Wide eyed wonders she told
from borrowed library books

Eyes wide opened never closed.

Thirty years later she told him
She was his mother.

It made sense.

Martin Swords June 2002

East Pier, Sunday Evening, 1959

From parish, pump, and townland
they came, with tired step and lonely walk,
sad resignation on their face, though he did
not know yet what resignation looked like.
He saw them hurry down the steps, or from
the train, brisk along the platform towards the boat.
Tall and straight, not old, not young, not stooped
nor beaten down, not yet.
Alone usually, or sometimes twos.
Heavy coated, black or brown market coats,
big buckled and broad belted, black boots
and baling twine. An old brown case held
with a leather belt.
Sometimes a woman on her own.

He held his father's hand, out strolling
down the pier, towards the band, the Army No. 1.
"They're the best", his father said.
Around half eight the Mailboat called
and a deckful of the best looked out.
A few waved.
The band played "Come Back to Eireann",
but they never came from Camden Town.
They left us and a great deal more behind.

He knew much later what he'd seen.
How much more than just a band,
a bandstand on a pier,
and a young boy waving at a boat

Martin Swords, October, 2009

Far From Athy

Pat told stories of old times, living in digs
in Athy, working on the roofin' for aul' Hammond.
Me with my booklearning piped up
"I heard of Athy,
'And look! a barge comes bringing from Athy
And other far-flung towns mythologies.' ",
lines from the canalbankpoet.*
"Bet he never saw it in the lashing
rain", Pat observed dryly.
No. Nor I had never seen it his way,
from a cold slate roof breaking galvanised
tacking nails with the long ripper,
and only the price of two pints in his pocket,
till Friday.

He was glad for me that I hadn't.

Martin Swords   May 2009

i.m. Pat Swords 1915 - 1978
On His Birthday 1st May

*From
Lines Written On A Seat On The Grand Canal, Dublin,
"Erected To The Memory Of Mrs. Dermot O'Brien"
By Patrick Kavanagh

As the hymn always reminds me, it was indeed

Joyful and Triumphant

Christmas, I remember,
Was the only time the fire was lit all day.
Da lit it real early with twists of the Evening Press,
Bits of broken wood, and coal brought from the
Backyard in the ashbucket.

The room was warm, flickering.
Once a year smells of Nutmeg, Spice and
Stale Guinness mixed with coal smoke, Pine,
And White Pudding.
Everything was lit up, for breakfast!

Red and white chains of crissed crossed crepe
Hung from light to ceiling corners.
Cards on the mantle, holly berries over the picture
Of The Big Fella', and The Sacred Heart.
And the Christmas Tree had
Cottonwoolballsnow.

The path was frosted white on the way out to the lav.
I rode my big wheel tricycle, squeaky, on the lino.
"Triumph",
Was written in old fashioned silver
Letters on the red metal bars.
And I was five, and Full of Joy.

It was happy and warm that
Christmas, I remember.

Dec. 2005   Martin Swords   Tiglin

Kathleen's Child Song   # 3

Freezing in December
Walking in the park
Thrown out by a Mother
For loving in the dark

Frightened by the changes
Uncertain of the facts
Soon to be a Mammy
Will he then come back

Why can't they love me
Can they not be true
All I know is when you're born
I'll be true to you

Waiting for the time to come
Fearful love and pain
With the babe, together, face
The world with pride again

Why can't they love us
Have they not love for two
All I wants a Mother's wish
Life, and love, and you

Sisters Pray for guidance
Say it's for the best
But Mother Superior doesn't know
A baby at the breast

I will keep my baby
I will, come what may
I will see him walk into
A bright and loving day

Kathleen's child is bonny
This child is fair of face
Kathleen's child is born of love
Love is no disgrace

Kathleen's child is bonny, bonny fair of face
Kathleen's child is born of love, love is no disgrace

Martin Swords   2006

One Day in Mind

(Findlater Street 1959)

The sound came faintly, growing
As he slowly worked the street.
A gentle song of unrequited love
Sung true to note in a voice
That once was strong.
The lilting rolling song matched
By his lolling rolling gait, moved closer.
The Streetsinger came calling
Once or twice a year.
Never asking, never begging,
Just singing, hoping, trusting.
Closer now his face reflected
Hardship, the ups and downs, and downs
Of life lived hard.
In someone else's shoes and shirt and tie,
Clean but tired and faded.
He wore his broken heart
On his shabby shiny sleeve.
The song moved on and faded
As he worked his way back down the other side.
Then stopped.
Looked at his meagre coins,
Walked sad slow steps away.

Another street. Another song.

We never knew his name but we remember.
Did he recall Findlater Street,
A young boy holding out a single shiny shilling.

He gave us more than we gave him.

Martin Swords, February 2000

One Road to Riches

And what did you do Daddy?

I played when I should have earned.
I scoffed when I should have learned.
I sat alone and thought when I should have worked.
I wrote too soon when I should have read,
and I looked away
when I should have seen what's wrong.
I ran when I should have fought
and I walked away when I
should have stood for right.

But I dreamed
and saw beauty in the ordinary things.
Imagined all was well
when it was not
but saw that it could be.

And what did you make Daddy?

I think I made a happy family.
And I made you, sons.
I hoped for you both
that you would dream as well.
See, and make beauty in your lives,
brighten the lives of others
and be rich without riches.
Be happy and bring happiness with you.

That's all I think I did.

Martin Swords   February 2000

Searching for a Father

For Kathleen

The story still unfolds.
The clues keep coming slow
of how a lovely lady loved,
thought loved in turn, and
loved the life she gave, to me.

She deserved better than the
suave and polished man
who fled, his pleasure taken.
Soft words, soft promises
were all he left to see her through

The dark and wintry nights of nineteen fifty.
She struggled through the cold
of shame and scandal. A time
when those who never loved
said love was bad and shameful.

Shame on them. What would
the neighbours and the family think?
Only a very few thought
to take her in
to give the girl a home
to give the child a brother.

Fifty years have passed and
people ask why keep on looking.
I have been greatly loved,
two mammies and a fairy story life
of warm and tender care.

I do not search for love, I could
not have more. But like a
mountain that must be climbed, because.
I need to know because he was
there and then was gone.

Martin Swords, December 1999

Song for Willie.
And Tommy.
And Ned.

i.m. Corporal William Byrne

'A' Company 1st Battalion King's Royal Rifle Corps
Born 1893 - KIA 27 October 1914
First Battle of Ypres, in Flanders Fields

We might have held you
If we had met
We might have helped allay
The fear that came too often
Until that fateful day
We might have offered comfort
We might have shed a tear
We might have heard it said
We'll not forget our comrades
Like Willie and Tommy and Ned

But you were there
And we are here
We came to find you Willie
We came though very late
We found you all together
Writ on Menin Gate
Little we did compared to them
Not found among the Fallen
But named among The Dead
Willie and Tommy and Ned

The bells of Ypres once shattered
Pealed a reluctant joy
At Eight O'Clock
Like poppies we stood long
The Last Post played in silence
The Last Post was your song
We who are blessed to remember
In remembering keep alive
So many, so terribly many dead
Like Willie and Tommy and Ned

Willie we remembered.
We found your name,
Perhaps your place of rest
Among comrades dead and gone.
With thanks and pride
We heard your song
We prayed for all the dead
But would that we had rather heard
The Song of Life resounding
For Willie and Tommy and Ned

Martin Swords, 27 October 2014, Ypres and Wicklow

Written to commemorate the 100th Anniversary of the Death- in-Action of
Corporal William Byrne. The occasion marked in a special way by the
presentation and laying of a personalized Poppy Wreath as part of the
Official Commemoration Ceremony at

The Menin Gate, Ypres, and playing of The Last Post, 27th October 2014
Presentation group and wreath laying party comprised three direct relations of Corporal William Byrne – 'Willie' –Russ Mansfield, John Goggins, Martin Swords – for all, an honour.

May he and all who died in the war of 1914 – 1918, Rest In Peace.

This dedicated poem was written partly at
The Menin Gate, Ypres, 27 October 2014, and later out walking dogs in the woods of Tiglin, County Wicklow, Ireland

The Holy Holocaust of Ireland, of Peter, James and John

Peter's growing in his mother.
She doesn't know she's pregnant.

James is in the leering look of George.
Uncle George thinking of young Molly.

John is in Pass Maths.
In the womb of a young girl doing the Leaving.

Peter's in the sacristy.
The priest is shouting shame at his mother.

James is in Molly's big belly.
They're in the kitchen saying the family Rosary,
waiting for the car.

John is nearly born.
His mother failed the Leaving with the upset.
Don't mention that shame either.

Peter's in his mother's arms.
They're looking from the gate up to the grey stone Home.

James and Molly, in Uncle George's car.
Heading for the nuns, somewhere far away where no one
knows Molly. Or George.

John is with his Granny.
In a parlour. In a convent. Under The Sacred Heart.
Waiting for a holy nun to take him.
Granddad's in the car outside. Listening to the hurling.
It's Sunday.

Peter's in tears.
In his wet nappy. In his metal cot. Near the window. His next cot companion, beside the window, is in a fit of coughing.

James is in the basket.
On the weighing scales, his weight OK, just.
He's in his mammy's thoughts and prayers. Always.

John is on the nun's list.
There are lots of names on the nun's list but John's name is near the top.

Peter's in a coma.
Beside the window now, he hasn't woken. For days.

James is in a blue blanket, all wrapped up.
His mammy thought she'd still be holding him. But she's not. She's upstairs at the long window screaming his name, crying hysterically. He's in the Ford Anglia. Soon he'll be in Ranelagh.

John is in Milwaukie.
He's warm, and fed, and sleeping. In a house his Mother could never dream of, or would ever know. Ever. His mother is in bits.

Peter's mammy's in a bad way.
Manchester, in a squat. Red Biddy in each hand. Not long now. She'll never hear or read about the angel's plot, the big tank, the eight hundred. Just as well.

James's mammy's in the convent still.
Scrubbing, serving, broken. She likes the new glass window of the holy children in the chapel. Sister Myra Anaesthesia put it in with money from America, they said. She likes the light, but she can't see through it. She feels attracted to it, she doesn't know why.

John's mammy's in New Jersey.
Older now. Looking. Always looking. Back home someone found a certificate where a baby's name was changed. 'Maybe this is it, maybe this one', she thought.
John is a doctor in Denver now, he knows nothing.

The Holy Holocaust.
The Holy Holocaust of Ireland, of Peter, James and John. And their mammies. No daddies.

Martin Swords   June 2018   'Kathleen's Child'

The Pint Half Finished

i.m. Pat Swords

A slow pint, Vincent, please'.
The words silently mouthed.
Pat sat down, anticipating.
Breathless after the walk to Walters
He lit a Player to recover.
The black pint, the creamy head,
the giant first swallow. Grand.
At home with friends and the
price of two pints. Easily contented.
A kind of chat, sign language,
The voice and half the throat removed.
They knew his ways in here. The friends.
Then like a light gone out, collapsed and gone.
A little fuss. A hushed quiet. Respect.
They knew. The men among men.
The life full lived and the pint half finished.
Later Mae cried, hysterical at the news.
'You never came back to me Pat'.

Will you ever forget the night Pat died,
And the pint half finished.

Martin Swords   1999

The Mother of No Child

For Mary Swords, who adopted me.

You were the mother of no child,
but yet a mother just the same.
Adopting both the child and natural mother
opened a door of happiness
for them if not for you.

Taken from school to keep your
family safe you missed the chance
of talk and learning.
A First in pots and pans and cleaning,
the school of life has many different honours.

Rearing the child, working when you
could on other peoples floors and halls
expecting little and rarely getting more,
the family held together.

The child was not your own.
We only know it now
the hope and sorrow
that your life combined.
The real mother always there.
We all held back the hugs and kisses,
the real love you should have got returned.

The story told too late
to say a proper thank you
to share the pride and
anguish that was yours.

The mother of no child
but yet a mother.
I know you better
now you're gone.
I know your joy and sorrow.
I know enough to thank you.

Martin Swords   December 1999

Two Tickets

They loved you always, Frankie
your old soft shoe, top hat and cane.
Half forgotten romance
and the distant passion of their younger days
Mae and Kathleen remembering, in middle age,
in love with your moonlight ways.
Their days were full of cleaning, minding, washing
my two Mammies, scrimping, saving, to
send me on my way,
you brought a colour to their tired
gray lives, on black and white TV.
Sunday Nights at the Palladium, top of the bill
you held their hands, you sang their song
you carried them away

But I was busy getting on,
Rushing, winning, promoting this, promoting me.
I saw the poster from my company granada
'Frankie Vaughan at the Olympia'
I'll make a note, I'll make a call, they'll love it.
I did nothing, let the moment pass,
no time to think of others on the ladder to success.

Now both are gone and now
I know how little I gave back, how little thought.

Two tickets never bought still haunt me
No night with Frankie for the ones who mattered.
The ladder lead to tinsel.
The good I might have done now scattered.
There in that other great Palladium
They're waiting for your turn.
"This one's for Mae and Kathleen", please Frankie,
say and tell them thanks, from Martin.
They'd love to see you Frankie
It would really make their day.

Martin Swords   April 1999

A Soft Hardship

"Go round and get an egg for Daddy's tea".
Out into the dusky evening
round the corner to Fitzel's.

That magic grown up shop
filled with smells for memories.
The big red slicer, offering
the fatty meat to the sharp
round blade, slicing the
smell of smoky streaky bacon.

And Jacobs' biscuits
in rows of sloping boxes,
glass lids offering temptation
beyond the power of young boys.
And Ling hanging from a hook.
Hard, like a wooden fish.

The egg appeared, wrapped
in a twist of news. The precious
message, safe delivered home
appeared again fried, sat on fried
bread for Daddy's tea. The good boy
got a soldier for his troubles.

Recalled years later for my own two
sons, a would-be tale of hardship.
David and Mark, the supermarket children,
could not imagine buying one egg,
much less imagine not having the price of two.

"And were you poor then"
asked the boys. In spirit we were never
poor. In other ways we were only an egg
wrapped in newspaper away.

Martin Swords   October 1999

*When we lived in Dalkey we sometimes brought Kathleen to the
house in her wheelchair, for lunch or dinner.
She got to see The Dalkey Fox visiting the front garden
a few times which she loved.*

The Dalkey Fox

    1

Brave furtive fox,
Decended from a line of
Dalkey fox of old
To this sad state.
Thin, scrawny shadow
Of your former self,
hunting through the gardens,
Stalking bins and refuse sacks
For scraps of Chicken Kiev,
Marks and Spencer meals
And Chinese takeaway.

You takeaway a living stealing quiet
The lean leftovers of the Dalkey diet

    2

Your home is in the brambles
On the last site left for sale.
The site more valued than
Your life and mine together.
You soon will be evicted, take
Your chances to survive
The JCB that clears the site,
That helped you stay alive.

Homeless in Dalkey's not the worst disgrace
You could be homeless in a less expensive place.

3

The Dalkey Short Arse Fox
We cruelly called
When you had lost your tail.
What caused your brush with Death
A Merc, or Masseratti?
You get run over
By a better class of Death round here,
But still you die.

They drive too fast, they make the engines roar
The Dalkey Tiger Pups bring death up to your door

4

When you are gone
As surely you'll soon be
We'll miss you calling in the night
The Dalkey Fox we thank you for your visits,
The owners of the site
Will never know you as we did
It is their loss, and yours.
You were condemmed to live and die
On real expensive real estate nearby.

The Des Res. in the brochure will be theirs not yours
Former foxes homes will get a mention on the
Dalkey Walking Tours

5

Our children will remember you
And tell their children too
About the Dalkey Fox who used to call.
Cruel life, cruel fate,
You should be wild in Wicklow
With your children at your heel
In mountain streams and moorland
In fields of pheasant, living foxy life for real

Not dying slowly in this most expensive place
A victim of the market in Dalkey's booming and
inhuman race

Martin Swords   August 1999

Chasing the Girls at Sandycove

Mary and Carmel and Clair
Hiding in the bushes wanting to be found
In the little park at Sandycove
Hoping the boys will come round

It's not too far along the seafront
Head towards Joyce's Tower
The little park before the harbour
Among the trees and bushes our early teenage bower

Raging hormones race within the girls and boys
As we ran and were caught among the bushes
Run slow, make sure to catch each other
Kissing and fleeing full of blushes

Not knowing why but yet compelled to play
This game of growing up unplanned
Chasing, catching, kissing
Driven by feelings we did not understand

Ann and Jane, Rachel and Alison
Wanting to be caught
John and Dec, Pete and me, not letting on
Our hearts were thumping in this uncertain game
Chasing the Girls at Sandycove
Driven by unknown urges as yet unnamed

Martin Swords   November 2019

You can read more of Martin's Poems on his poetry page,
https://martinswordspoetry.wordpress.com/

For other books of poems and stories by Martin look for:

- Glendalough Calling
- A Letter to Mary
- Five by Five by Five
- The Last Little Wood
- Story?
- Ramblings On My Mind

https:.//www.amazon.co.uk/

And from Wicklow Writers Group:

- Anniversary
- Short
- The Long Stone and other treasures
- Tales of Patrick and Doris

https:.//www.amazon.co.uk/

Say 'hello' on Facebook
Look up Martin Swords on Facebook

Video for Kathleen's Child

glendaloughartsnetwork

Page Notes

Printed in Great Britain
by Amazon